quilted
symphony

A FUSION OF FABRIC, TEXTURE & DESIGN

GLORIA LOUGHMAN

C&T PUBLISHING

Text and Artwork copyright © 2010 by Gloria Loughman
Artwork copyright © 2010 by C&T Publishing, Inc.
Publisher: Amy Marson
Creative Director: Gailen Runge
Acquisitions Editor: Susanne Woods
Editor: Lynn Koolish
Technical Editor: Sandy Peterson
Copyeditor/Proofreader: Wordfirm Inc.
Cover/Book Designer: Kristen Yenche
Production Coordinator: Zinnia Heinzmann
Production Editor: Alice Mace Nakanishi
Illustrator: Aliza Shalit
Photography by Tony Loughman unless otherwise noted.
Photography of author's hand drawings by Christina Carty-
Francis and Diane Pedersen of C&T Publishing, Inc.
Published by C&T Publishing, Inc., P.O. Box 1456, Lafayette,
CA 94549

Library of Congress Cataloging-in-Publication Data
Loughman, Gloria, 1949–
 Quilted symphony--a fusion of fabric, texture & design /
Gloria Loughman.
   p. cm.
 ISBN 978-1-57120-660-2 (soft cover)
 1. Patchwork. 2. Machine quilting. I. Title.
 TT835.L694 2010
 746.46'041--dc22
                                        2009023380

Printed in China

10 9 8 7 6 5 4 3 2

Acknowledgments

Thank you to C&T for undertaking the publication of this book. Special
thanks to my wonderful editor, Lynn Koolish, for bravely signing up for a
second book with me. Once again, your calmness and skill have helped me
tremendously over the past year.

I will always be grateful to my parents, Florence and Jack, for their encour-
agement and proud endorsement of my work.

I would also like to recognize my students, who have been as excited about
colors and shapes as I am and have encouraged me to publish my ideas
and techniques. I would especially like to thank the students whose quilts
appear in this publication. You have inspired me!

Thanks go also to our daughters, Amanda, Sarah, and Rebecca. Though
they all lead very busy lives, their unconditional emotional and practical
support continues to validate for me the wonderful fulfillment of
family life.

And, most of all, I would like to say thank you to my husband, Tony, who
finds a way to make almost everything possible. His total support for my
career, his logic, and his love has sustained me throughout the 40 years of
our marriage. I have really enjoyed our quiet times working on this book
together. Building a new house, having to move, and living in temporary
accommodations with our belongings in storage have been some of the
challenges we have faced while writing and photographing the material for
this book. Together, we made it!

Dedication

I would like to dedicate this book to my beautiful grandchildren, Charlotte,
Declan, Malachi, Lucy, Benjamin, and baby Robson, who is due to arrive
about the same time as this book. May your spirit of creativity be fostered
and nurtured so that you can meet whatever challenges lie ahead.

I would also like to dedicate this book to Associate Professor John Collins,
a dedicated breast cancer surgeon who has looked after many of the
members of my family over the past 21 years.

Contents

INTRODUCTION . . . 4

DESIGN AND COMPOSITION . . . 6

Elements of Design . . . 7

Principles of Design . . . 9

Where to Look for Inspiration . . . 15

Getting Started with a Design . . . 16

Design Process . . . 21

COLOR . . . 22

The Color Wheel . . . 23

Describing Color . . . 24

Color Schemes . . . 26

CONSTRUCTION . . . 33

Drawing the Design . . . 34

Preparing the Base . . . 36

Making the Segment Patterns . . . 36

Making the Segment Background . . . 36

Decorating the Segments . . . 37

Removing the Stabilizer . . . 37

Positioning the Segments . . . 38

Invisible Appliqué . . . 39

Appliquéing the Segments Together . . . 41

Removing the Base . . . 41

SURFACE DECORATION . . . 42

Appliqué . . . 43

Piecing . . . 56

Feature Fabrics . . . 59

Beading and Braids . . . 60

PAINTING FABRIC . . . 61

Preparing to Paint . . . 62

Applying the Paint . . . 63

Gradations of Color . . . 64

Sun Printing . . . 65

Creating Textured Fabrics . . . 65

STITCHING . . . 66

Appliqué Stitching Options . . . 67

Decorative Stitching Options . . . 73

BORDERS, QUILTING, AND BINDINGS . . . 76

Borders . . . 77

Quilting . . . 79

Bindings . . . 80

STUDENT GALLERY . . . 84

PROJECTS . . . 89

Project 1: Simple Appliqué
and Foundation Piecing . . . 89

Project 2: More Detailed Appliqué . . . 92

Project 3: Mosaic Appliqué . . . 95

Project 4: Abstract Landscape . . . 98

RESOURCES . . . 103

ABOUT THE AUTHOR . . . 103

KIMBERLEY MYSTIQUE, 80″ × 88″ (203cm × 224cm), Gloria Loughman
Photo by Sharon Risedorph

Introduction

A few years ago I made a quilt called *Kimberley Mystique*, which was based on a remote region of northwest Australia. Rather than faithfully reproducing the scene, I made a decision to incorporate my love of pattern. So choosing images that could be easily recognized, the distinctive large boab trees, I played with patterns and shapes within the perimeter of their stately trunks.

I really enjoyed the whole experience of making this quilt—I loved playing with the colors, the textures, the shapes, and the patterns. This quilt went on to win Best of Show at my state exhibition and then the prestigious Australian National Quilt Award.

While teaching landscape classes both overseas and close to home, I had many inquiries about the techniques used to make this quilt: questions about the design process, the color choices, the fabric decoration, and the stitching techniques. I realized that there were many quilters who wanted to take that next step, to make something more abstract.

Talking to students, I discovered that many were afraid of the word "abstract" but had a keen desire to try something new. In art, the term "abstract" describes something that is not a true representation but relies on color and form to convey an idea or impression. Abstraction can be achieved through altering shapes, colors, or both. It can mean taking the process much further, to the point where the design is entirely about the essence of the chosen subject without regard to its physical appearance. Abstraction is usually an intellectual approach. The artist must select, modify, and manipulate the elements and design the surface of the image to express his or her response. Certainly a challenge!

So if you would like to experiment with patterns and colors and want to take that next step but don't know where to start, then this book is for you. Work through the design strategies, audition new color schemes, learn new stitching techniques, and go on to make your own interpretation of your chosen subject. Alternatively, use one of the patterns as the starting point for your first quilt; then, using this book as a resource, take the next step of designing your own stunning quilt. The information and techniques presented here will open up a whole new world of quiltmaking to you.

Circular lines of farm machinery

A variety of industrial lines

Circular shapes featured on agricultural machinery

Lines of a rusty wrought-iron fence

Rooftop lines

Combination of shapes in Venice

Design and Composition

Any quilt you make, whether it is traditional or contemporary, is an act of design. You are creating a set of marks, shapes, and colors that have a connection to each other. These days, many quilters realize the importance of design and want to learn more. Others feel overwhelmed and don't wish to venture down that track, but in fact they are intuitively using many of the key elements in their work.

For abstract quilts, design is very important because its elements, and the way they are manipulated, are the key to producing work that is eye-catching and powerful. Take a look at the various elements of design described here. They are the building blocks with which you construct your picture and the fundamentals that make your work interesting.

Elements of Design

LINE

A line is a path between two points. It can be thick or thin, wavy or straight, jagged or calm, simple or decorative. It can be horizontal, vertical, diagonal, or zigzag.

A line is implied when two shapes abut one another and thus become integral to piecing. Lines can define boundaries. They can divide or connect and help move the eye around a design. See the images on the previous page for examples of how lines contribute to designs.

Printed lines are often a feature on commercial fabrics. Lines can also be created by stitching and couching fibers.

SHAPE

Shapes are the areas created when a line or several lines meet to enclose a space. These shapes can be geometric, such as squares, circles, and triangles, or organic, such as leaves, shells, or fish. In a design, there should be a variety of shapes. They can be created by delineating the actual shapes or by defining the space around them, called negative shapes. Negative shapes or spaces can be very beautiful and sometimes create more impact than the original positive shape. Additional examples of how shapes influence design are on the previous page.

COLOR

As color is one of the most powerful and expressive elements in design, I decided it deserved a whole chapter of its own (pages 22–32). Color can evoke emotion and mood, convey temperature, and apparently even stimulate our appetites. It can be peaceful and calming, or energizing and stimulating. It can be intense or muted and is particularly important in abstract work.

VALUE

You can create a sense of space in your work by using value. Value is the lightness or darkness of a color, determined by the amount of white or black added. By changing the value, shapes can be made to look like three-dimensional forms. For example, with value changes, a circle becomes a sphere. The contrast between the lights and the darks enables us to portray shapes and figures that give our quilts visual impact. We will look at value in much greater depth in the chapter on color.

Boxlike shapes of buildings in Tenby, Wales

Arches and rectangles in Venice

Color-washed squares provide more texture and interest.

TEXTURE

Texture refers to the tactile quality of a surface. This texture can be actual or implied. Quilts are a tactile medium, and we often long to run our fingers across their surface. They also provide visual texture because of their patterns of color and shape. Textures can be subtle or bold; they can be qualities that are intrinsic to a particular fabric, or they can be added by the quilt artist through stitching or appliqué.

Variations of color can also produce visual texture that is completely independent of how the object would feel to the touch. Consider the subtle color variations of fruit and the mottled patterns of rust on a ship. In real life, shapes are rarely a single solid color. Usually there is visual texture because of the tantalizing color variations.

With this thought in mind, consider using a subtle print fabric or a combination of color-washed squares rather than a solid-colored fabric.

Shiny, tough texture of crocodile skin

Worn tiles in old city of Cairo, Egypt

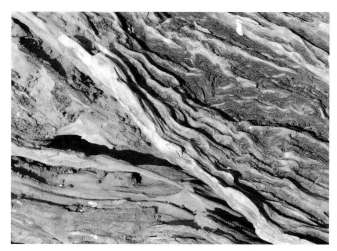

Coarse texture of bark

Lichen growing on rock face

Principles of Design

You have the list of elements that you can use to fill your design surface with lines and shapes, but you also must take into account some design principles if you want to compose the best arrangement.

HARMONY

Harmony is a sense of unity or oneness—a feeling that everything in a work belongs, with shapes, colors, textures, subject, and concept working together toward a single purpose. When looking at artwork, you usually try to make sense of what you see. You try to find relationships between the visual elements. When parts of what you see are too dissimilar and unrelated, the overall design of a piece does not have coherence and you lose interest.

There are a number of strategies you can employ to achieve harmony in your work.

Repetition

Harmony can be produced by repeating similar shapes, colors, edges, patterns, textures, values, lines, and so on. In an abstract design it can be tempting to randomly join disparate elements together, but for a design to be effective, all the elements must have a feeling of belonging together in some unified way. If any of the elements seem to disrupt this sense of unity, remove them.

Detail from *African Dreams* (quilt on page 33). Repeating many fabrics in an area makes them look like they belong.

Most often, repeated elements have more impact if they are used with some variation. Repeating shapes in different colors, values, or sizes will add visual interest yet still provide the harmony you are after.

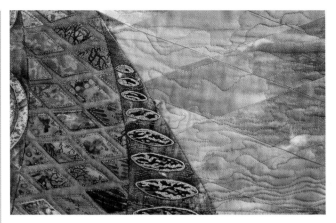

Detail from *Kimberley Mystique* (quilt on page 4). Repetition of diamond piecing in one section and diamond mosaic in another provides unity.

Detail from *Kimberley Mystique* (quilt on page 4). Similar colors flowing across surface create unity and harmony.

Detail from *Ancient Water Course* (quilt on page 66). Repeated shapes and colors provide interest and unity.

Objects that come in threes are intriguing.

Detail from *Kimberley Mystique* (quilt on page 4) shows how contour quilting across shapes unifies areas.

Linking

Grouping shapes together or visually linking various elements together will contribute to harmony across the design. Try overlapping shapes and linear arrangements to help the viewer see the design as a unified whole. Odd numbers are more interesting than even numbers. Things that come in threes, fives, and sevens are particularly intriguing for the mind. As larger groups of items are not taken in with a single glance, they can be less effective for visual linking. Elements that cross boundaries can help unify a design. Continuous quilting across areas may also provide a bridge to help link shapes together.

A BIT OF AFRICA MEETS THE OUTBACK,
35½″ × 28″ (91cm × 71cm), Heather Ridley

Odd numbers provide interest (sunbursts and kangaroos).

Quilting that extends over edge carries design into border.

CONTRAST

If all the elements in a design are similar, there may be unity but there will probably be boredom. Contrast, the exact opposite of harmony, surprises the eye, contributes excitement and tension, and relieves monotony. Try using a variety of similar rather than duplicate elements. For example, a mixture of reds, a variety of lines, or a selection of circles will produce the exciting kind of unity you wish to attain.

Size

Varying the size or scale in a design is important in achieving an interesting composition. The relationships between small, medium, and large lines or shapes help add impact to the overall design. Most quilters are used to thinking about scale when using printed fabric—small-scale or large-scale florals, for example. A quilt made of only tiny prints can look boring. A mixture of large, medium, and small prints or perhaps a mixture of stripes, dots, and patterns is varied and interesting.

There are other ways to vary the scale in a quilt. In the simplest terms, most good compositions have large spaces, medium spaces, and small spaces. A variety of sizes creates more visually satisfying relationships. Remember that background or negative space is a legitimate, important design element. If you don't want to fill in a large space with a solid piece of fabric, consider using a subtle, visually textured print or an area of pieced fabrics close in color and value, which your eye will combine and read as one space.

Detail from *Sunbaked* (quilt on page 81). Pieced diamonds provide interest but read as one background.

Old green door stands out against soft rosy-red bricks.

Colors

As mentioned earlier, similar colors add harmony, while complementary colors push away from each other, injecting energy into a composition. See page 27 for more on complementary colors.

There are a variety of elements to work with to create contrast, and you can use them in countless combinations. In addition to color and size, there are also contrasts in textures, edges, temperatures, surface treatments, fabrics, fibers, and so on.

Overuse of Contrast

It is possible to overuse contrast and bring a composition to the brink of chaos. You must keep the contrast under control or it will destroy any sense of visual harmony.

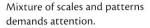

Mixture of scales and patterns demands attention.

Vivid red berries provide strong contrast to bright green leaves.

BALANCE

Creating balance is a key factor when planning a design. If a composition is balanced it will feel right. Often an intuitive aspect of composition, balance is about creating a sense of comfort and equilibrium. Whether the elements are distributed more or less evenly or arranged asymmetrically, the final composition should look visually balanced and pleasing to the eye.

Balance implies that the elements within a composition have a sense of weight. Large objects generally weigh more than small objects, and dark-colored objects weigh more than light-colored objects. The position of these elements is also critical. We unconsciously assume that the center of a picture corresponds to a fulcrum, or balance point. A heavy weight on one side can be balanced by a lighter weight on the other side if the lighter weight is located at a greater distance from the fulcrum.

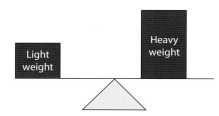

Heavy weight is balanced by lighter weight if it is further away from fulcrum.

A composition will lack balance if its components do not entice the viewer's eye to cross over a central axis. If all the visual activity is concentrated on one side of the composition, the viewer has no reason to look from one side to the other.

Achieving balance is a matter of adjusting the visual weight. If balance is created with visual elements identical in both weight and energy on either side of a central axis, then a symmetrical or *static* balance is achieved. If the balance is created with two elements that are not identical in weight and energy, then an asymmetrical or *dynamic* balance is achieved.

Symmetrical Balance

Symmetrical or static balance is quite familiar to quilters. It implies a sameness or uniformity on either side of the central axis. Quilts made with blocks in a grid arrangement are usually symmetrical by their very nature.

STEPPING STONES, 23½″ × 23½″ (60cm × 60cm), Gloria Loughman
This block quilt has symmetrical balance.

Asymmetrical Balance

Asymmetrical or dynamic balance is based on an uneven arrangement. It is when the elements are not the same on different sides of the quilt, but there is still a feeling of balance. This type of balance is accomplished in the way two children on a seesaw are balanced by one adult. This is pleasing to our aesthetic sense, but achieving this type of balance takes more skill and practice than does symmetrical balance.

Dynamic balance is achieved by adjusting the visual weight of the design components so there is enough variation to be interesting but not so much that the picture loses coherence. If the components are too dissimilar, an imbalance will

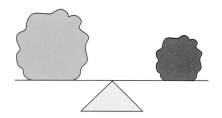

Large light-colored shape is visually balanced by small intensely colored shape.

occur. Size, color, texture, and many other components can be adjusted to create a visually exciting balance.
For example, a small, intensely colored shape can visually balance a large, light-valued one.

Positive space is where shapes are positioned, and negative space is the empty space around these shapes. The negative space balances the area that the elements occupy. Areas of a picture that contain nothing are important visual elements that provide balance in an image and allow the eye to rest.

By constantly evaluating your compositions, you should eventually come to a point where all the elements feel right.

Focal Point

Every composition should have one main area of interest, a feature that entices the viewer in and captures his or her attention because the area is so visually appealing. This spot is called the focal point.

A focal point can be created using a number of different techniques. It can be a strong contrast in value (for example, a light fabric next to a very dark one), a contrast in color (using complementary colors), a contrast in intensity, a hard edge, a gap in pattern, or an intersection of lines.

What attracts the eye is some sort of contrasting characteristic that makes an element stand out because it is unlike any other.

Lamppost positioned a third of the way across rather than in center

Placing the Focal Point

The focal point should be placed in a position that is a different distance from all sides of the picture.

Many artists and photographers use the rule of thirds, whereby a picture is divided into three sections, vertically and horizontally, and the lines and points of intersection represent places to position important

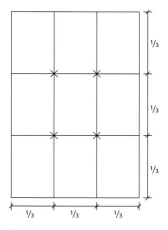

Position important visual elements off-center by placing them at intersections of grid.

visual elements. When creating a landscape, moving the horizon to the position of one-third is often more effective than placing it in the middle, where it will cut the work in half. But, it could also be placed near the bottom, below the one-third line. There is nothing obligatory about using the rule of thirds; it is just a starting point.

Direction

Because a viewer's eye tends to follow a defined path through a composition, try to make that path as interesting and as long as possible without creating an easy exit. Avoid shapes or strong lines that lead off the edge of the quilt; instead, include elements that lead toward the focal point.

Repeated marks, lines, shapes, colors, or tones can also act as arrows that direct the viewer's eye. For example, if a painting has vivid blue marks repeated

Detail from *Kimberley Mystique* (quilt on page 4). Arrowlike shapes act as pointers, directing the eye where they point.

in three places, perhaps describing a triangle, the eye will follow them, drawing an imaginary triangle in the process.

Movement

Horizontal shapes or lines give a feeling of peace and tranquility. Vertical lines or shapes imply strength and power. Diagonal lines imply movement and change. Consider the oblique lines of the crashing surf or windblown grass. Lines can express mood or emotion—a jagged line can describe aggression and anger, whereas a curved line feels slow and lyrical.

Gradation in color provides a gentle form of movement. Colors can be graded from light to dark, bright to muted, or warm to cool. You can unify contrasting areas by making a gradual transition between them or make a dull area more exciting with gradations of tone or color.

It may be that not all these elements will be present in a work. Sometimes one element will dominate, with the others playing a minor role. Often the ways in which these elements are used become characteristic of an artist's style.

Water lilies floating on flat surface convey stillness.

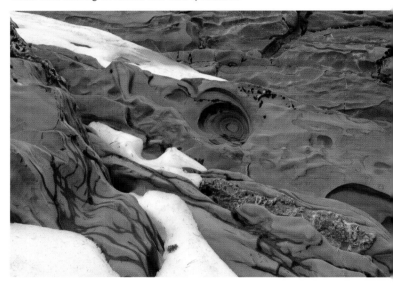

Diagonal lines and circles imply movement.

Spinning circles provide movement.

Still water with its reflections suggests tranquility.

Where to Look for Inspiration

Inspiration can be found just about anywhere, from the most everyday situations to the exotic. You just have to have a keen sense of awareness and an open, receptive mind. Look around you. Consider the possibilities. Sketch, photograph, and record potential images.

Different view of Africa

Colorful spectacle of Cairo market

Coastal view

Sand swirls

Out of gas in Namibia

Tide pools

Colorful canvas bags and rich aroma of spices in Cairo

Getting Started with a Design

There are many ways to begin an abstract design. You can begin with something recognizable, such as a scene or object, or start with a simple beginning, such as a collection of lines and shapes. I use the following methods to break up a design into individual segments; these segments are the starting point for the construction of my quilts (see page 33).

METHOD 1: BEGINNING WITH A DOODLE

Take a sheet of paper, and begin to draw. Break the background up into simple spaces. Try to let the pencil move lightly and freely across the work. Try curved and straight lines. Let some shapes be small and others large. Try to cover the whole page with different-sized shapes.

Now try filling in the shapes with more lines and patterns. Anything goes. The main thing is to just let the design develop naturally so you can feel a sense of flow. Develop more elements, but leave some shapes untouched. Continue until the design feels balanced. Your design might take on the form of simple figures or faces or other recognizable images, but it need not refer to anything real—it can be a unique and expressive design that deserves to be explored further.

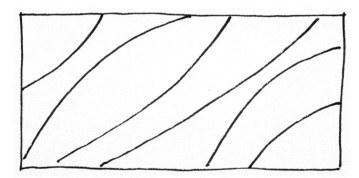

Break up background into simple spaces.

Fill in with lines and patterns.

METHOD 2: STARTING REALISTICALLY

An alternative starting point is to begin with a natural object. Start in a realistic way, and then extend lines, repeat shapes, mirror images, and so on.

Original close-up photo of elephant

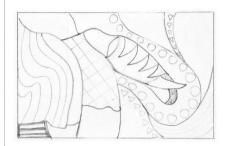

Design based on elephant photo

Choose an object that interests you, and make a basic drawing.

Begin with a few leaf shapes.

Extend some of the lines to the edge of the page. This will immediately disguise the original outline and create another set of shapes to which you can add color, pattern, texture, and lines. These different treatments of the shapes will change the overall effect.

Extend some lines, and add patterns.

Repeat the original drawing, and change the way you fill the shapes. See what effect this has on the composition.

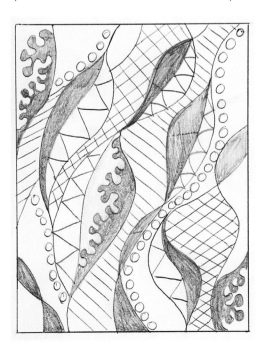

Filling shapes with different patterns changes design.

By repeating the image several times until you hit the edge of the paper, the whole background becomes covered with interesting shapes ready to fill in with patterns. Try overlapping and changing the size of the original image to create even more designs, or use the mirror image of the original design.

METHOD 3: ALTERING SHAPES

Begin with a drawing of your chosen subject and then change some of the lines. An example would be to curve or angle all the original straight lines. Add extra lines. Fill in some areas with patterns that disguise the original outline.

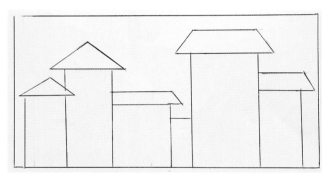

Draw some buildings.

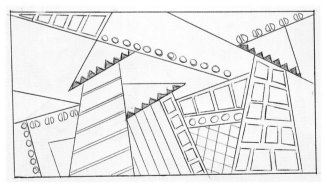

Change some lines and fill in with angled lines and patterns.

METHOD 4: USING PHOTOGRAPHS

Sift through your photographs until you find one you really like. Make a full-page black-and-white photocopy, and then use this as a reference to make a simple line drawing. It may be that you use just some of the lines in a stylized way to give a feel of the location or subject. It is best to draw freehand rather than tracing, as this adds to the abstract nature of your work. Try to be selective as you do this, extracting the main lines and shapes.

Old farm machinery provides inspiration.

Pattern for abstract design

To convey a real sense of the place, include patterns and other textures that you found on location, if appropriate.

These photos were taken on a visit to the Romsey Abbey Church in the United Kingdom. The collage of photos provides a wonderful source of inspiration for an abstract design.

Inspiration for quilt based on Romsey Abbey Church

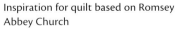

Design based on church photos

METHOD 5: CUTTING UP DRAWINGS OR PHOTOGRAPHS

Begin with a drawing or photograph. Make a number of full-page photocopies, either black-and-white or in color. Cut one of the photocopies into strips. Now reassemble the strips. They can be in any order and at the same or different heights. Paste the strips down onto another sheet of paper so you have a permanent record to refer to.

Rocky Mountains vista in Canada

Cut image into strips, and rearrange levels and order.

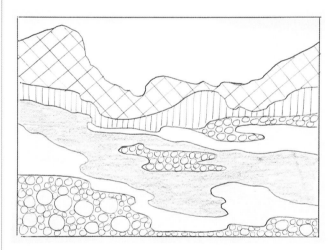

Trace abstract design from strips.

Repeat the process using the other photocopies. Change the size of the intervals and/or their final positions. Try leaving some out or adding spaces to fill in.

METHOD 6: EXTRACTING A SECTION

Here, the starting point is again a photo or drawing, but this time we are going to lift a section from it and develop a design from the resulting arrangement of lines. As the image is not shown as a whole, it will appear to be abstract.

BUTTERFLY, 19″ × 15″ (48.3cm × 38.1cm), Catherine Redford
This quilt was made by extracting a section from a photo.

Once again, prepare a full-page photocopy. Try out several compositions—one drawing can be the source of many interesting designs. Use L shapes to select rectangular or square sections of the original image. Have a good look at each section, and see what is visually appealing.

Original photo of cathedral in Venice

Selected segment provides wonderful design source.

Original photo of old wagon wheels

Use L shapes to find best view.

Selected segment is great start for design.

METHOD 7: USING FABRIC AS A STARTING POINT

You may have been saving a very special fabric that you want to highlight in a quilt. Pin this fabric to your design wall, and let it talk to you. Look at the shapes. Consider whether they are a source of inspiration for the background design. Think about where you will use the fabric in the quilt. This feature fabric will probably stand alone in various segments but will be supported with shapes, patterns, colors, and lines in other segments. The Australian theme quilt *Ancient Water Course* (page 66) highlights a very special hand-printed fabric with circular designs in orange and turquoise that look like wheels.

METHOD 8: USING A THEME

Have you been collecting a group of fabrics based on a theme and haven't come up with a way of using them in a quilt? A collection of Japanese fabrics was the inspiration for *The Apprentice Kimono Maker* (page 49). I stylized a simple drawing of a kimono, altering some of the lines but still trying to keep the essence of the shape. I then filled the shapes in with patterns and colors, careful with my placement of lights and darks to ensure that the basic design was still evident.

Design Process

Everyone works in a different way. One of my friends just starts cutting fabric, and the design gradually evolves. For most of us, though, it is a good idea to sketch out ideas on paper. If you achieve a design that is pleasing on paper, it is almost guaranteed to be equally successful as a quilt. You don't have to stay exactly with the design. Try to remain open and observant, as sometimes wonderful and unexpected things happen, especially when paint is involved.

DESIGN WALL

Use a design wall to audition your composition and colors. Stand back and be critical. Make sure you are happy with each stage of the process. Check that the design is working out as planned. Ask yourself questions, such as, Do I need more contrast to see important shapes? Are there any distractions on the edges that lead the eye away from the focal point? Enjoy the journey rather than rushing to finish.

note *Develop your own sense of observation and evaluation. Visit quilt shows and other exhibitions; note which quilts or paintings you find most appealing, and spend some time thinking about why they demand your attention. In competitions, look at quilts judged to be winners; appraise them in terms of design and color. Can you establish why they are award winners? Look at the quilts that win Viewers' Choice awards. Why are they so popular and visually pleasing to lots of people? By asking yourself these questions, you can learn a great deal about design and the use of color, and go on to develop your own skills in these areas.*

Beautiful old painted houses in Venice

Intriguing old cart in marketplace in Cairo

Celebration of color and pattern in Venice

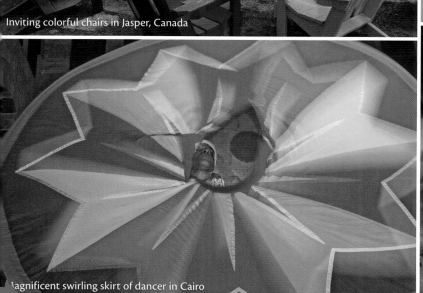

Inviting colorful chairs in Jasper, Canada

Magnificent swirling skirt of dancer in Cairo

Stunning colors of the microscopic *Botrylloides*
Photo courtesy of Keolab

Color

Vivid red of *Pentagonaster* on ocean floor

"Only those who love color are admitted to its beauty and immanent presence. It affords utility to all, but unveils its deeper mysteries only to its devotees."

—Johannes Itten,
The Elements of Color

Color, of all the design elements, has the greatest emotional impact and fully deserves a chapter of its own. We can't live without color. Like music, color enriches and enhances our lives. Color helps us express our emotions and can stimulate our imagination. Understanding color and its power helps you create something special, be it peaceful and calming or bold and exciting. Color demands response.

Color combinations are an endless and fascinating source for exploration and discovery. From electric complementary mixes in which the colors sing, to harmonious families in which each color supports the others, to simple but strong visual contrasts, all have an important role to play. A basic appreciation of how color works can really help when you are creating a color scheme for a quilt.

There are so many beautiful and varied colored fabrics on the market today that perhaps the sheer breadth of choice available can be confusing and even, at times, intimidating. Some people have an intuitive color sense. Others experience success with color after studying and, in a sense, dissecting the work of others. Look around you. You will find inspiration from sources you could never imagine. Plants, vegetables, sea creatures, paintings, restaurant menus, in-flight magazines, pieces of pottery, furnishing fabrics, spools of variegated thread, tiles, textiles and buildings from other cultures, shipyards, and industrial areas—the list is infinite, but you must have your eyes and soul open to respond.

The temptation to create what you see rather than what you feel can be overcome by planning your color scheme before you start selecting fabric. Indeed, the color scheme for *Kimberley Mystique* (page 4) was inspired by a painting of an ancient ship. I loved the striking combination of the golden yellows, oranges, and reds with the beautiful turquoise and decided that I would use that scheme for my next quilt—not the true colors of the Kimberley area but my own interpretation.

By studying some of the following color schemes, you will begin to gain an understanding of the effect colors have on each other. Interestingly, the more you know about color and understand structured color schemes, the more individual and personal your color choices become. Your work becomes richer and more powerful as you proceed with more confidence and knowledge.

The Color Wheel

A color wheel is a very useful reference tool to help you identify wonderful color schemes. The colors on the outside of the circle are pure, bright colors and those on the inside are lighter, duller, or darker.

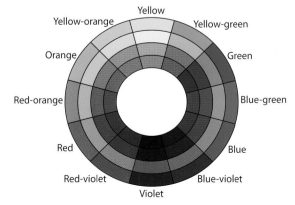

Color wheel

Describing Color

There are three ways to describe color: hue, value, and intensity.

HUE

Hue is the name of the color and refers to the wedge of the color wheel that contains a single hue with all its color variations. For example, the blue hue family contains color choices such as powder blue, sky blue, ice blue, gray blue, cornflower blue, and navy blue, among others. Every color belongs to one of the hue families on the color wheel.

Some members of blue hue family

VALUE

Value is the relative lightness or darkness of a color. The value of a color has nothing to do with the color itself but is a comparison of the color to a scale of grays that ranges from white to black. Using value wisely can go a long way toward making a design hold together. The proper arrangement of lights and darks will help the eye move freely through the work, ensuring a strong composition.

One way to see value is to squint your eyes, as this makes it easier to see light and dark rather than color—squinting restricts the part of the eye that sees color and leaves the part of sight that sees only value. This becomes easier with practice. Some artists like to view their work in a mirror to check whether the composition is working—this way the artist is seeing the work with a fresh eye.

It is interesting to note that the seventeenth-century artists Rubens and Rembrandt worked with color and value separately. They would start out building their paintings using only white, various shades of gray, and black. When this was dry they would apply thin coats of transparent color over this base, ensuring that the values in the painting worked.

Notice that the value of cool colors is darker than the value of warm colors. The color on the color wheel with the lightest value is yellow. In a design, light values tend to jump out more than dark colors. A little yellow goes a long way because as well as being a warm color, at its most intense it is also the lightest color in value.

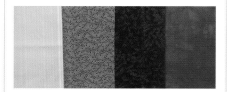

Mix of colors: yellow, turquoise, blue, and red

Same color in black and white, showing their values

When a design contains only very dark and very light values, the dark colors make the light ones look lighter and duller, and the light colors make the dark ones look darker and duller.

A composition that uses the middle value scale for most of the values, and includes very light and very dark values as accents, works well. The middle values act as a link or bridge for the dark- and light-value accents, enabling all the colors to be highlighted without appearing lighter or darker than they actually are. This is the most widely used value composition by far, and one that is easy to use. A feeling of richness, strength, and balance can be evoked using this combination.

Lights and darks

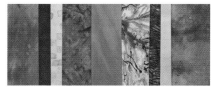

Mediums with lights and darks as accents

THE BLUE PEBBLE PATH, 23½″ × 28″ (60cm × 72cm), Penny Wells

Accents of light and dark work well with middle values.

If most of the values fall in the darker range, the feeling can be theatrical and dramatic but can also be heavy and somber when very dull colors are used. Adding more contrast is key to making the piece more exciting, but again, you need to add both medium and light accents. Remember that you need the medium values to provide the connection.

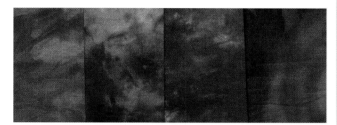

Dark color range

Color range is more exciting when mediums and lights are added.

The best way to learn about value is to work in black and white. Choose just one color plus black and white (this limited palette is called a monochromatic color scheme), and work with these three elements for a while. With this scheme, value is the essential element and color cannot be used as a crutch. Value must work or the composition will disintegrate.

STUDY IN GREY, 33¼″ × 26½″ (84.5cm × 67.3cm),
Dawn Wakelam Hunt
Photo by Keith Hunt

Of the three ways to describe color, value is the most important because it is the first characteristic of a design that can be seen from a distance, and it remains important at close range.

INTENSITY

Intensity, also called chroma or saturation, is the relative brightness or dullness of a color. A color is at its most saturated or intense when nothing else has been added to it—when it is at its purest. Intense colors are more eye-catching in a design than those that are less intense.

Intensity can be decreased in several ways.

- **Tinting:** Adding white to a color will make it less intense as well as lighter in value. The more white you add, the lighter and less saturated the color becomes. To create tints using paints, begin with white and add small amounts of color until you achieve the desired intensity. That way you won't have to add your whole jar of white paint to achieve the desired effect.

- **Toning:** Adding gray will also decrease the color's saturation. The more gray you add, the less saturated the color becomes.

- **Shading:** Adding black to a color will make it both darker and less saturated. When black is added to a cool color, it will appear darker but still appear to belong to the same hue family. When black is added to a warm color, however, the change is more pronounced. Yellow begins to look more like olive green, and orange turns brown. When painting, begin with the pure color and add small amounts of black to obtain the desired shade.

- **Adding a color's complement:** Adding the color that is opposite to it on the color wheel will also make the original color duller. The two original pure colors neutralize each other and create a dull gray.

To maximize effect, you should use a range of color saturation. The colors should neither be all pure nor all gray. Save the pure or high-intensity colors for the focal point.

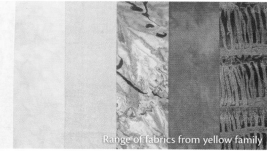

Range of fabrics from yellow family

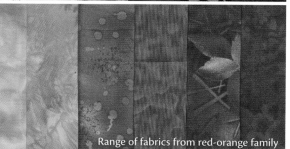

Range of fabrics from violet family

Range of fabrics from red-orange family

Monochromatic quilt—red family

Monochromatic scene in Namibia

Color Schemes

Choosing a color scheme can be quite daunting, especially with the seemingly infinite variety of beautiful fabrics available today. As colors are usually seen together with other colors and not in isolation, understanding their relationships to one another will help you make more successful color choices.

The color palettes here are for you to experiment with. Try some of them, and along the way you'll develop your own eye for color.

MONOCHROMATIC COLOR SCHEME

When only one hue family is used in a design, it is called a monochromatic design. Remember that there are many color possibilities within one hue family. Color can be lightened or darkened in value by adding white or black, or dulled in intensity by adding gray or other colors.

Obviously, value is the most important aspect of this color scheme. Generally, the strongest contrasting areas will attract the eye.

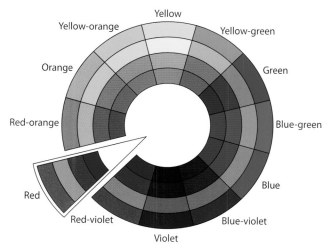

Wedge of hue family from color wheel

COMPLEMENTARY COLOR SCHEME

Complementary colors are directly opposite each other on the color wheel. Complementary colors are a dramatic and powerful combination. We often see this scheme in nature. The red and green of rhubarb leaves, violet flowers with dazzling yellow centers, burnt orange earth and brilliant blue skies. Sometimes the scheme is dramatic and exciting, and at other times it is quite subtle and can almost be overlooked. Complementary colors are beautiful, especially when a variety of their tints and shades are used. When blended together, they create additional colors that work beautifully with the original colors.

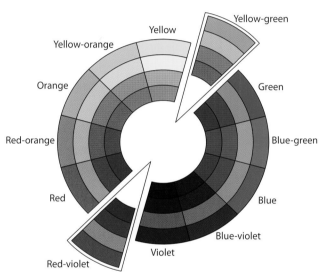

Red-violet and yellow-green are complementary colors.

Complementary pairs, when placed next to each other, will intensify each other and appear electric. For example, when yellow is placed beside violet, the yellow will look more intensely yellow and the violet more intensely

Beautiful violet and yellows of *Botrylloides*
Photo courtesy of Keolab

violet. By choosing other variations of the hue family, such as tints, tones, and shades and complementary blends, you can moderate the intensity of the contrast to your liking.

A sample of the beautiful range of blended colors obtained by combining complementary pairs is shown here.

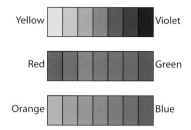

When you plan a design using a complementary color scheme, make sure that one color is dominant. If both colors have equal visual power, there will be visual competition and the design will suffer. The viewer's eyes will jump from one spot to another, not knowing where to rest. By using a fraction of a complementary color as a sharp accent, you get a more vibrant and stunning effect.

Certain pairs of complementary colors have unique qualities.

- Red and green are probably the easiest to work with, as these colors are similar in value.

- Orange is the warmest color and blue is the coolest color on the color wheel. Orange tends to dominate because of its warmth, so it can be a challenge to maintain a balance between these two colors. Using less-intense hues of this pair of complements can be a solution.

- Yellow and violet can be difficult when both colors are at their most intense because they differ so much in value. But by experimenting with different values for each color you can achieve a good balance.

Complementary colors—
yellow-green and red-violet

Orange with blue   Red-violet with yellow-green   Yellow and violet

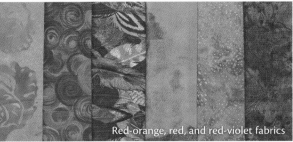

Red-orange, red, and red-violet fabrics

Extended scheme of orange, red, and violet

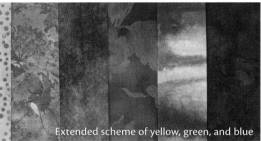

Extended scheme of yellow, green, and blue

Analogous colors—yellow-orange, yellow-green, and blue-green

ANALOGOUS COLOR SCHEME

Analogous colors are hue families that are found next to each on the color wheel. "Analogous" means closely related, and often three and even up to five adjacent colors can be used together for this scheme. This scheme depends on a key color that connects the family, thus providing harmony. This is probably the most popular color scheme among quilters, as it is beautiful and easy to use. Many exquisite colorings in nature superbly illustrate this harmony. Fabric designers often use an analogous palette, especially for soft furnishings.

An analogous color scheme can include any color within the wedge: tints, tones, and shades as well as the hues themselves. You can change the values, proportions, and intensity of the colors for different effects.

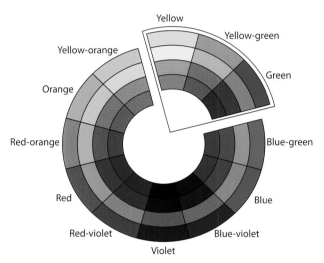

Analogous wedge of yellow, yellow-green, and green families

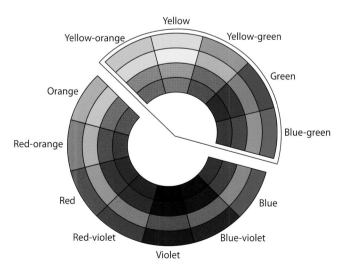

Extended analogous wedge

When using the extended wedge, not all the colors need to be included.

SPLIT COMPLEMENTARY COLOR SCHEME

Basically, this is an analogous color scheme with one contrasting color. Begin by choosing three analogous colors that will convey the dominant mood of the design, then take the middle color and select its opposite, or complement, to be used as the contrasting accent color. You can then choose to include the middle color or leave it out.

Eye-catching flowers in split complementary colors

This is my favorite color scheme, as I feel the accent color makes all the difference. It is harmonious and rich but still has contrast and strength.

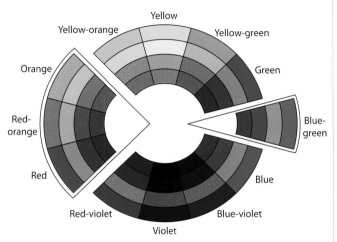

Split complementary scheme with middle color included

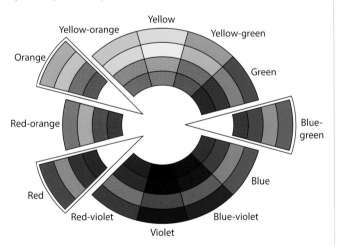

Split complementary scheme with middle color left out

Split complementary—red, red-orange, and orange with complementary blue-green

With middle color: yellow-green, green, and blue-green with red

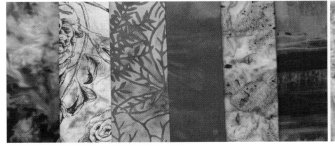

Without middle color: red and violet with yellow-green

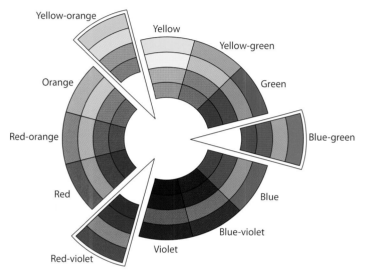

TRIADIC COLOR SCHEME

Returning again to the color wheel, the basic idea for this scheme is a firm relationship between colors that are equal distances from each other. This color scheme is quite different from the previous color schemes, as these colors have little harmony and do not intensify each other. The success of this scheme usually depends on one color family having a major role. One of the other families becomes the secondary player, with the third having a very minor role. Remember, you can also use their tints and shades as well as mixing the colors together. There are only four combinations of triads.

Triad colors—yellow-orange, red-violet, and blue-green

Wedges of colors form triadic color scheme.

Blue, yellow, and red

Violet, orange, and green

TETRAD COLOR SCHEME

This color scheme is made up of two sets of complementary colors. They can form a rectangle or square on the color wheel. The square tetrad will promise a very striking palette, as the colors are as far away as possible from each other on the color wheel. These schemes can be quite complex, because you are dealing with families of warm and cool colors, and, if used in equal amounts, the warm hues will dominate. Once again, decide on a dominant color, and then have fun filling in the rest.

Fabrics from yellow and violet plus blue and orange families

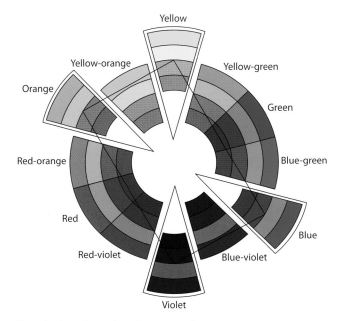

Tetrad color scheme based on rectangle

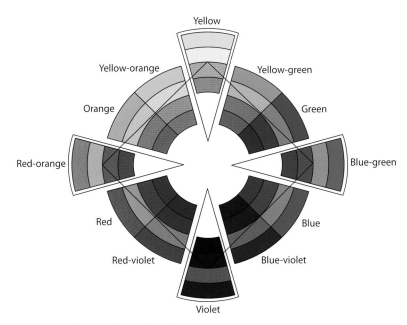

Tetrad color scheme based on square

Tetrad colors—yellow and violet with blue and orange

Beautiful flowers showcase tetrad colors.

HEXAD COLOR SCHEME

This scheme uses three pairs of complementary colors. The hue families can be equidistant on the color wheel or three analogous colors with their complements. The equidistant hues can look somewhat like a rainbow unless the intensity and value are decreased. The analogous hues and their complements give a range of color that is harmonious but versatile.

Hexad colors—blue-green, blue-violet, red-violet, red-orange, yellow-orange, and yellow-green

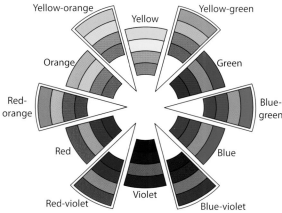

Hexad color scheme—equidistant

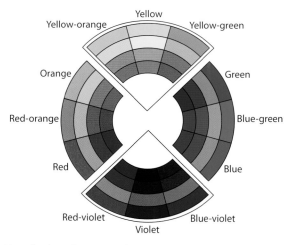

Hexad color scheme—analogous

So many different palettes to choose from! Certainly personal preference will come into play. Thankfully, we all have different tastes. Remember that there is no right or wrong color scheme. It is just that some are far more appealing and set a mood better than others. Take time to experiment and play with some of these color schemes. Try making a series of small quilts using different palettes. You will certainly develop your own eye for color along the way.

Keep your color wheel handy as you select your fabrics. It is a wonderful reference tool.

You should also visit museums and galleries and look at how other artists approach color. Learn from the masters!

The 3-in-1 Color Tool is a color-planning tool that can help you choose effective combinations (see Resources, page 103).

Fabric samples highlight equidistant color scheme.

Fabric samples show second equidistant color scheme.

Construction

AFRICAN DREAMS, 38″ × 49″ (96cm × 125cm), Gloria Loughman

My construction process is based on making the individual segments and then appliquéing them together on a base of tear-away stabilizer. The advantage of this technique is that the segments can be embellished with intricate stitching while they are still small and easy to maneuver under the sewing machine.

Drawing the Design

One of your first decisions will be the size and shape of your project. It can be a rectangle, a square, a circle, or an irregular shape. A major consideration will be the space where the finished quilt will hang. You may want to sketch out your design in a smaller scale before drawing it out full size. Alternatively, you can proceed straight to the full-size drawing. You don't need to know all the answers before you begin. The section Getting Started with a Design (page 16) has suggestions on where to start.

1. Draw the outside edges of your design on paper.

2. Experiment with curved lines to break up the background into a number of segments. It is important to have variations in the size and shape of the segments.

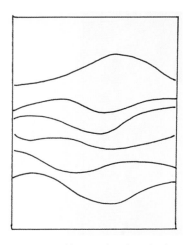  

Draw curved lines to break up background.

If you have a theme in mind, incorporate your ideas in the design of the background segments.

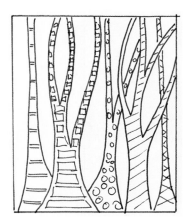 

Background segments based on themes

3. Begin to fill in the background segments with shapes and patterns. The drawings at this stage can just be ideas. Accurate drawings will come later in the process. Keep in mind that some of the areas will showcase a single fabric and so will remain empty at this stage. Others will be pieced using regular piecing techniques (page 56) or foundation piecing (page 58).

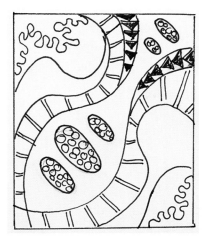

Fill in background with shapes and patterns.

4. It is now time to number each background segment. Number the segments in the order in which they will be applied to the tear-away stabilizer base at a later stage. Usually the best option is to start with number 1 in the middle and then work out.

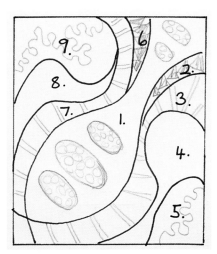

Number segments in order in which they will be appliquéd to base.

As the segments overlap when appliquéd, the correct order for application will allow sharp points to be managed easily.

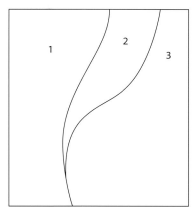

Correct order allows sharp points.

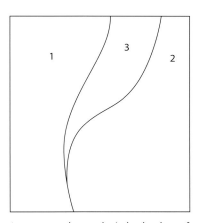

Incorrect order results in both edges of point of segment 3 needing to be turned under.

5. Draw a small arrow toward each edge that will be turned under.

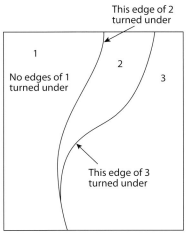

Arrow points to edges to be turned under.

Preparing the Base

Cut a piece of tear-away fabric stabilizer slightly larger than the pattern. Use a pencil to trace the outline of the main background segments and the borders onto the tear-away stabilizer base.

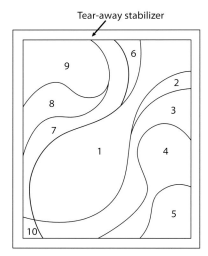

Create base from tear-away stabilizer.

For a larger quilt, overlap the edges of the tear-away stabilizer, and tape or pin them together.

Making the Segment Patterns

Use a pencil to trace the outline of the segments onto the dull side of freezer paper. Include the segment numbers. At this stage, you are tracing the lines directly from the pattern, and you do not need to leave seam allowances on the freezer paper. Cut out these shapes.

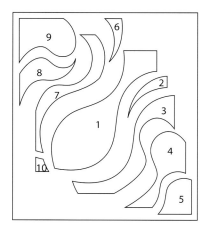

Cut out freezer paper shapes.

tip If your freezer paper is too narrow, you can overlap sheets and use an iron to join them together. Better still, use the Ricky Tims' Extra-Wide Freezer Paper to avoid this problem (see Resources, page 103).

Making the Segment Background

note *Not all segments need a background fabric. With some decorating techniques, such as creating a background made of squares or diamonds (pages 56–57), or foundation piecing (pages 58–59), the background is created as part of the surface decoration.*

1. Choose the background fabric for each segment. Iron the freezer paper pattern for each segment onto the *right side* of your chosen fabric. Cut out each segment with a ½″ (1.3cm) seam allowance all around the outside edge of the freezer paper. For segments that will not be embellished, stitch a row of straight stitching ⅛″ (3mm) out from the edge of the freezer paper, all around the segment piece.

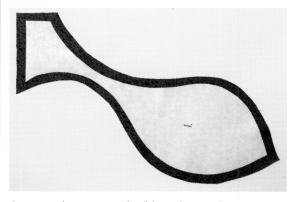

Cut out each segment with ½″ (1.3cm) seam allowance.

For segments that need to be stabilized for embellishment, follow the steps below.

2. Pin a piece of tear-away stabilizer to the back of the background fabric, leaving the freezer paper in position.

The tear-away stabilizer is slightly larger than the background fabric.

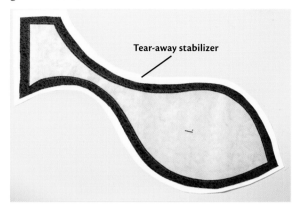

Add tear-away stabilizer to back.

3. Stitch a row of straight stitching ⅛″ (3mm) out from the edge of the freezer paper, all around the segment piece. This stay stitching will define the space to be decorated and embellished, filled with patterns and shapes. As it is slightly larger than the finished segment, it allows for the segment edge to be turned under and the stay stitching to disappear underneath or be overlapped by another segment.

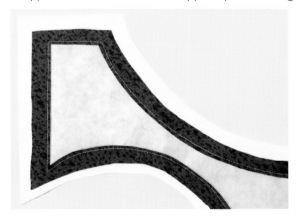

Stitch ⅛″ (3mm) out from edge of freezer paper.

4. Remove the freezer paper.

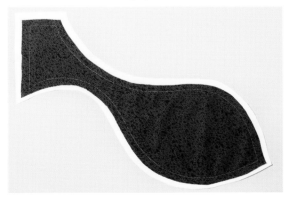

Remove freezer paper.

Decorating the Segments

There are many different ways to decorate and embellish your quilt. You can let the fabric speak for itself in some areas and use the decorating and embellishing ideas that are described in the next chapter for other areas.

■ For segments that will feature appliqué, make the segment background as outlined in Steps 2–4 in Making the Segment Background (page 36), then decorate with your chosen appliqué shapes.

■ For segments that feature piecing, including foundation piecing, follow the steps on pages 56–59.

As the embellished segments are completed, pin them to the design wall. It is important for them to hang vertically so that you can view the finished segments from a distance.

Completed segments are ready to be joined together.

Removing the Stabilizer

Once all the segments, including the appliquéd and pieced segments, have been completed, remove the tear-away stabilizer from the individual segments. You will find that the tear-away stabilizer will tear more easily in one direction than the other. Small scissors or tweezers can be useful. Small amounts of the stabilizer can be left in areas of close stitching. Do not put too much stress on the stitching when you are removing the stabilizer.

Positioning the Segments

1. Place Segment 1 on the tear-away stabilizer base, using the drawn lines as a guide. The outline stitching on the segment should sit just outside the drawn line on the tear-away stabilizer. Pin this segment in position.

Segment 1 in position on base

2. Trim the edge of Segment 2 that is to be turned under to a ¼″ (7mm) allowance. This edge will have been marked with an arrow on the drawn pattern. Clip if required (for curves), turn under this edge, and press to the back. The row of stay stitching should just disappear under the edge. A schematic of this process is shown here.

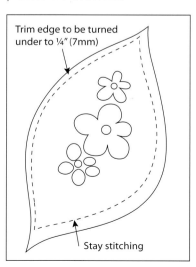

Trim turn-under allowance to ¼″ (7mm).

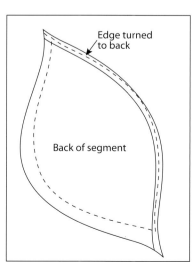

Stay stitching should disappear to back.

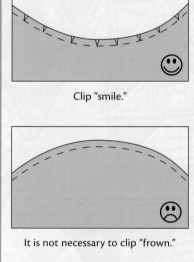

3. Pin in position, overlapping Segment 1. Pins should be placed 2″–3″ (5cm to 8cm) apart, perpendicular to the edge.

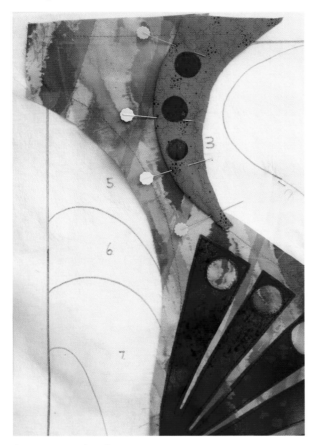

Segment 2 overlaps Segment 1.

Invisible Appliqué

The next step is to join Segment 2 to Segment 1 using an invisible appliqué stitch on your sewing machine. Invisible appliqué uses the sewing machine's blind hem stitch. Set the stitch selection to blind hem stitch, consulting the machine manual if necessary. The blind hem stitch does 4–7 straight stitches on the right, then a zigzag to the left. On some machines you can mirror image the stitch to sew the opposite way.

Hints for Mastering a Truly Invisible Appliqué Stitch

1. It is important to have the stitches sit right in the ditch, so use a foot that is open at the front or a clear or open-toe appliqué foot to give you the best view. The open-toe embroidery foot (page 67) is a good choice.

2. Thread the top of your machine with a good-quality monofilament or polyester invisible thread. I recommend MonoPoly from Superior Threads or Wonder Invisible Thread from YLI. In the bobbin, use a neutral thread or one that matches the fabric color. It is preferable to blind hem stitch using a finer bobbin thread such as The Bottom Line from Superior Threads.

3. Change your needle to a size 60/8 or 70/10. The size 60/8 needle makes a smaller hole, which will be less noticeable. The monofilament thread is very fine, and it will fill only a small hole—hence the preference for finer needles. Take care, though, as they are easily snapped in half if you pull your work too quickly out from under the needle.

Threads for blind hemming

MACHINE SETTINGS

The settings for the invisible blind hem stitch will vary depending on the brand of your machine. For Bernina and most Janome machines, reduce the stitch width to a little narrower than 1. It should be just wide enough to barely catch two or three threads of the top fabric. Also, adjust the stitch length to a little under 1. If too much space is left between the stitches, there will be gaps along the edge. The zigzag stitches should be ⅛″–¼″ (3mm–7mm) apart. The setting for most Husqvarna Viking machines is stitch length 0.3 and stitch width 1.5. For some models of Pfaff, you have the option of tricking your machine into stitching a narrower width by pressing the twin-needle button. Although it is not actually using a twin needle, the machine thinks it is and takes only a half-size bite into the appliquéd layer. The settings for some models of the Pfaff are length 1, width 3, and twin-needle button on. Some of the latest machines have a set appliqué stitch. Get out your manual and look at the options. The best stitch is the one that is almost invisible.

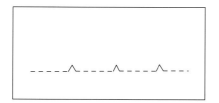

Blind hem stitch

Appliqué stitch

The tension will probably need to be adjusted because of the very short stitch length being used. Begin by reducing the top tension slightly, that is, turning the top tension dial to one number lower than normal. On the Bernina, thread the bobbin thread through the finger on the bobbin to tighten up the bobbin tension. If the bobbin thread is still coming through to the top when you are stitching, then loosen the top tension.

Check your settings on a sample placed on tear-away stabilizer. Only the zigzag stitch will bite into the top layer. If you see any of the bobbin thread coming through to the top, then you need to decrease the top tension further. If you have reduced the top tension all the way down and can still see the bobbin thread on the top, then it is time to take out the bobbin case and tighten the tiny screw on the side. Turn the screw to the right the equivalent of 10 minutes on the clock. Replace it in the machine and try again. If you are using a finer bobbin thread than normal, it is a good idea to tighten the bobbin case at the beginning. (See pages 67–69, Satin-Stitch Appliqué, for more on bobbin tension.)

Invisible blind hemming

Stitches are virtually invisible, even on closer view.

Appliquéing the Segments Together

1. When you are happy with your invisible appliqué stitches on a practice sample, sew along the pressed-under edge of Segment 2 with the zigzag stitch just catching the edge of the Segment 2 fabric and the straight stitches sitting on Segment 1. As these segments are pinned to the tear-away stabilizer, you are stitching through this base as well.

2. Once Segment 2 is stitched in position, repeat the process, adding the subsequent segments in order. Change the bobbin thread to match the background fabric as necessary to ensure that the stitches are invisible.

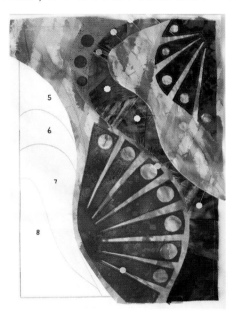

Add segments in order.

Removing the Base

When all the segments are in place, remove the tear-away stabilizer base prior to adding borders and quilting. (See Removing the Stabilizer, page 37, for tips on this step.)

Remove tear-away stabilizer base when all segments are in place.

PLAYING ON THE SURFACE, 18½″ × 25″ (47cm × 64cm), Gloria Loughman

Now the fun begins. There are many decoration options listed here, but I am sure you can come up with many more of your own. If there is a particular technique that you have developed or enjoy using, chances are that it can be incorporated as part of the surface decoration on your quilt.

Appliqué

Many of the decorations involve appliquéing motifs or edge treatments in position on the background fabric segment.

Appliquéd motifs

Appliquéd edge treatment

APPLIQUÉ MOTIFS—UNIQUE SHAPES

If the motif is symmetrical and doesn't need to be reversed to use fusible web, trace the original drawing from the pattern onto the paper side of paper-backed fusible web. Cut out the drawn shape, adding a ¼" (7mm) allowance around the edge. Iron the paper-backed fusible web to the back of the motif fabric.

Cut out the motif on the drawn line. Remove the fusible paper backing, and position the motif on the segment background fabric. If you are happy with the result, iron it in position.

Iron paper-backed fusible web to the back of the fabric, cut out shape, then iron the motif in position.

> **tip** Always check the manufacturer's instructions, as some paper-backed fusible webs need a dry iron for maximum adhesion.

> **tip** Some of the more recent paper-backed fusible webs, such as Steam-A-Seam, are adhesive and allow you to position the motif without ironing. If you are not happy with the result, the piece can easily be removed and repositioned elsewhere.

If the image needs to be reversed (so it comes out oriented correctly as a fused element), use either a lightbox or a window to transfer the image from the *back* of the drawing to the paper side of the paper-backed fusible web. Alternatively, you can trace the image onto the freezer paper pattern and use this as a guide for cutting, as described on page 44:

1. Draw or trace the design onto the freezer paper pattern, and cut it out with an allowance around the edge of the drawing.

2. Choose the fabric for the motif, and iron sufficient paper-backed fusible web to the back of the fabric.

3. Iron the cut-out freezer paper motif to the *right side* of the fabric, making sure you line it up with the paper-backed fusible web on the back.

Iron freezer paper to fabric backed with paper-backed fusible web.

4. Using the drawing on the freezer paper as a guide, cut around the shape. Remove both the paper backing of the fusible web and the freezer paper, and iron the motif in position on the background fabric of the segment.

Cut around shape, using freezer paper as guide.

Remove freezer paper.

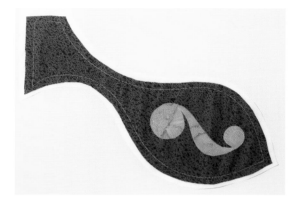

Iron shapes in position on background fabric.

APPLIQUÉ MOTIFS—REGULAR SHAPES

Regular shapes such as circles can be drawn directly onto the paper side of the paper-backed fusible web. Thread spools, drinking glasses, plates, and other appropriate circular items found around the house can be very useful for drawing circles. Place them in position on the freezer paper pattern to check whether the size is appropriate. A compass gives you a full range of circle sizes.

Iron the paper-backed fusible web to the back of the selected fabrics, and cut out along the drawn lines. Position the shapes on the segment background fabric.

Designs within circles are eye-catching and can provide a great focal point. Draw the outside circle to size, then add additional fabrics to create wonderful, complex designs.

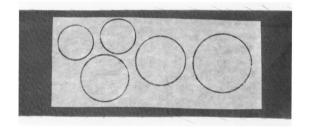

Iron paper-backed fusible web to back of fabric, cut out, and fuse in place.

Circles provide interest and excitement in a design.

APPLIQUÉ MOTIFS—SPIRALS

Spirals can be drawn directly onto the paper-backed fusible web, but to avoid a mirror image, follow the techniques described in Appliqué Motifs—Unique Shapes (page 43).

1. To create a spiral, begin by drawing a circle on the paper-backed fusible web. This circle should be the size of the outside edge of the spiral. Begin to draw in the second line, coloring in the spiral as you proceed.

2. As you come around toward the starting point, move your pencil from the inside line to the outside line, and continue this line inside to make the second ring of the spiral.

3. Coloring in as you go, continue both lines in toward the center.

4. When you are almost at the center, draw a small circle shape on the end.

5. Iron the paper-backed fusible web to the back of the spiral fabric. Cut out carefully along the drawn lines. You will be rewarded with 2 spirals.

6. Remove the paper from the paper-backed fusible web, and carefully position the spirals on the segment background fabric. The spirals can be positioned centrally or offset over the edges. Iron the spirals in place.

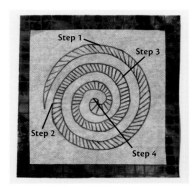

Draw spiral.

Iron fusible web to back of fabric, cut out spiral, and fuse it in place.

APPLIQUÉ MOTIFS—FLYING GEESE

1. Draw the triangles on the freezer paper pattern by drawing the base lines first, changing their direction as they proceed around the curves. Find the midpoint of the base, and draw in the other 2 sides of the triangles.

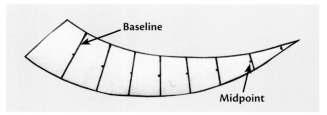

Draw base lines of triangles, and mark midpoint of base.

2. Number the triangles in order.

3. Iron the freezer paper onto the right side of the triangle fabric. Iron paper-backed fusible web to the wrong side of the fabric, behind the freezer paper.

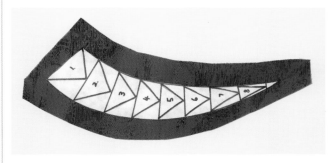

Iron freezer paper guide to triangle fabric.

4. Cut out each individual triangle. After removing the freezer paper and fusible web backing paper, place each triangle in position on the segment background fabric. Iron in position.

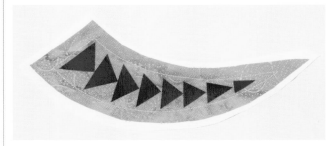

Cut out triangles, place triangles on background segment, and fuse them in place.

EDGE TREATMENTS

Fascinating shaped edge treatments can be appliquéd to some of the segments, providing definition and interest. These shapes can be continuous or broken. Many examples have been provided, and no matter which you choose, follow this technique for accurate and easy construction.

1. Prepare the segment fabric background as described on pages 36–37. Draw the edge treatment design onto the freezer paper pattern.

Prepare segment and draw design on freezer paper.

2. Remove the freezer paper from the segment background, and roughly cut out the design.

3. Cut a piece of paper-backed fusible web slightly larger than the freezer paper guide, and iron this to the *back* of the edge trim fabric. Iron the freezer paper guide to the *front side* of the trim fabric.

Iron freezer paper to right side of trim fabric.

4. Cut out the decorative edge trim, using the freezer paper as a guide and adding a ¼″ (7mm) seam allowance along the side matching the segment seam edge.

Cut out trim with seam allowance along segment seam edge.

5. Peel off the freezer paper and the paper from the paper-backed fusible web.

6. Align the edge trim in position on the front of the background segment, overlapping the stay stitching.

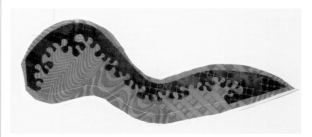

Align trim in position, overlapping stay stitching.

7. Press the trim in position, and stitch along the decorative edge to hold it in place. Free-motion stitching is the obvious choice if the design is complex. If the shapes are less intricate, a narrow satin stitch can give more definition.

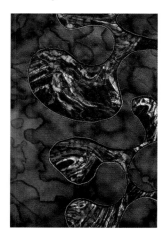

Free-motion stitch around intricate shapes.

Detail of *Kimberley Mystique* (quilt on page 4). Use narrow satin stitch around larger shapes.

tip Variegated threads look wonderful if you have developed your free-motion stitching techniques. If you are just starting out, it may be wiser to stay with a matching color thread.

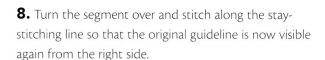

8. Turn the segment over and stitch along the stay-stitching line so that the original guideline is now visible again from the right side.

Another continuous edge treatment

Broken edge treatment

SHADOWING

An extremely effective technique is to create a shadow effect around one or more of the appliqué shapes. This can work well for both single motifs and edge treatments. Cut a second appliqué image in a darker- or lighter-colored fabric, and offset it from the original shape when positioning the images on the quilt. You will need to make a second freezer paper guide for the second image.

Offset and iron in place.

BRODERIE PERSE

Some stunning motifs and edge treatments can be created taking advantage of commercial prints. Look for interesting designs that can be cut out and used to decorate the segments. Always apply fusible web to the back of the image before cutting it out.

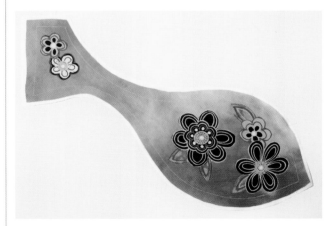

Cut out shapes from commercial fabric.

Multiple shapes can be fused along an edge to create unique and exciting designs. Position the fused shapes to overlap the stay stitching on the edge of the background segment.

Fuse multiple shapes along edge.

MOSAICS

A very effective surface decoration involves creating a mosaic pattern on one or more of the segments, resulting in a tile effect.

Detail of mosaic patterns from *African Dreams* (quilt on page 33)

Mosaics—Choosing Fabrics

When choosing your fabrics, remember that you need contrast between the background and the tiles. Often a dark background will really highlight the colors of the tiles,

but lighter backgrounds can also work well. Revisit your color choices for the whole quilt, and consider including these colors in the mosaic to create unity (page 9). The mosaic sections are often some of the larger areas, so harmony will be important.

If you cut the tiles from one fabric, a patterned or multicolored fabric is usually the most effective. A fabric that gradually changes color creates drama and is very appealing. See the painting techniques on pages 61–65 to create your own unique fabric. Patterned fabric also works well, as each tile tends to be different but in sync with the rest.

You may also use many fabrics, which is more time consuming, but the dramatic results make it worth the effort. Choose a group of fabrics that blend well or perhaps change color gradually. Incorporate fabrics featured in other areas of the quilt, creating that important harmony across the quilt surface.

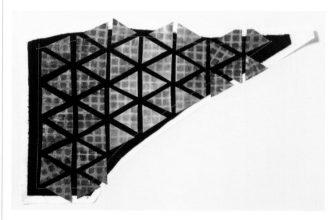

Mosaic tiles cut from one fabric

Mosaic tiles cut from group of fabrics

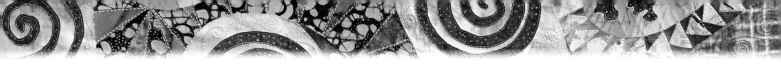

THE APPRENTICE KIMONO MAKER, 23½" × 32" (60cm × 82cm), Gloria Loughman

Mosaics—Tile Shapes

The tiles can be cut in a regular or irregular pattern to fit comfortably within their boundary. They can completely fill in an area or partially fill a prepared background segment.

Kimono quilt detail. Black segment completely filled in with tiles.

White segment partially filled in with tiles

Mosaics—Regular Tiles

Tiles can be cut as squares, rectangles, triangles, diamonds, or other regular shapes.

Cutting Squares and Rectangles

Squares and rectangles can be cut quickly, easily, and accurately using a rotary cutter, ruler, and cutting mat. Cut a piece of paper-backed fusible web, and iron it to the back of the chosen fabric(s). Remove the paper backing from the web, and position the fabric, fused side down, on the cutting mat. Cut accurate squares and rectangles to your chosen size using a rotary cutter and ruler.

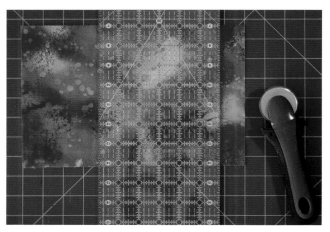

Cut accurate squares or rectangles using rotary cutter, ruler, and mat.

As the backing paper has already been removed, these tiles will be ready to be placed on the prepared background segment.

> **tip** Try using a paper-backed fusible web, such as Lite Steam-A-Seam 2, which allows you to temporarily stick tiles in place. It is repositionable until fused in place with an iron. When using this product, leave backing paper in position when cutting.

Cutting Diamonds

You can cut diamonds in any size—just make sure they are in proportion to the size of the area to be covered. The cut measurements for average sizes are given on page 57. The following shows how to rotary cut accurate diamonds.

1. Cut a sheet of paper-backed fusible web, and draw a straight line ½″ (1.3cm) in from the bottom edge. Position your ruler so the 30° ruler line is on the drawn line. Draw a second line along the ruler's edge.

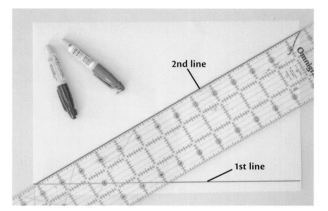

Position 30° line along drawn line, and draw second line.

2. Turn the ruler over, and position the same 30° line along the initial drawn line. Draw a third line along the ruler's edge.

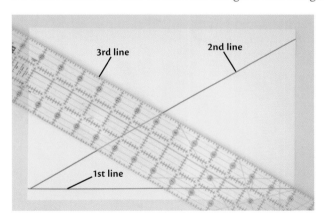

Position 30° line on back of ruler along original drawn line, and draw third line.

3. Draw 2 sets of parallel lines 1¼″ (3cm) from the second and third drawn lines until the whole grid is filled in.

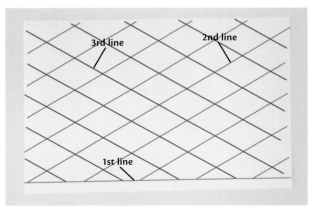

Draw parallel lines until grid is complete.

4. Iron the paper-backed fusible web to the back of the selected fabric, and, following the grid lines, cut out the diamond shapes with a rotary cutter or scissors. If you are using multiple fabrics for the diamonds, first the grid can be cut up, and then sections can be ironed to the backs of different fabrics. Remember to remove the backing paper from each tile before it is positioned in place on the segment background fabric.

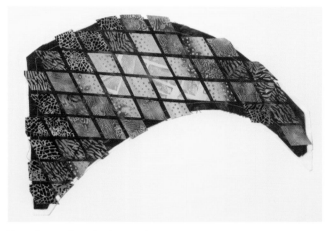

Fuse diamonds on background.

An alternative to drawing the grid on paper-backed fusible web is to trace around individual diamond templates that are commercially available in multiple sizes. These are very useful if you are just cutting one or two shapes from many different fabrics. Trace the diamonds onto paper-backed fusible web, fuse them to the back of your fabric, and cut out.

Commercial diamond-shaped templates are an alternative.

Cutting Triangles

A similar technique can be followed for creating a grid of triangles on paper-backed fusible web.

1. Cut a sheet of paper-backed fusible web, and draw a straight line ½″ (1.3cm) in from the bottom edge. Position the ruler so the 60° line is on the drawn line. Draw a second line along the ruler's edge.

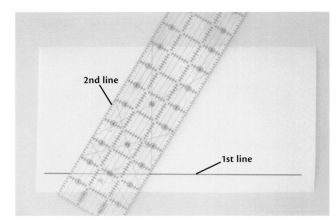

Position ruler so 60° line is on initial drawn line.

2. Turn the ruler over, and position the same 60° line along the initial dawn line. Draw a third line along the ruler's edge.

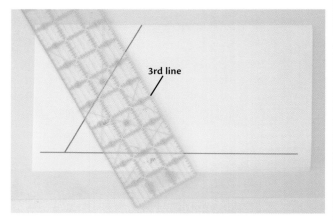

Turn ruler over, and position 60° line on original drawn line.

3. Draw 3 sets of lines spaced 1¼″ (3cm) apart, parallel to the original 3 drawn lines, to create a grid of equilateral triangles.

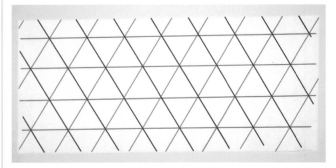

Draw parallel lines to complete grid.

4. Fuse this grid to the back of the selected fabric or fabrics, and cut out the triangles.

Arranging Tiles

Prepare the background fabric for each segment to be tiled following the directions for embellished segments in Making the Segment Background on page 36.

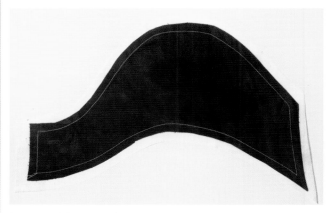

Segment with stay stitching

Place the fabric tiles in position on the segment background fabric, trying to keep the distance between them uniform. A ¼″ (7mm) gap works well, but this may need to be adjusted based on the size of the tiles. Begin in one corner, and gradually fill in the area. At times you will need to position the tiles over the stay stitching to provide good coverage.

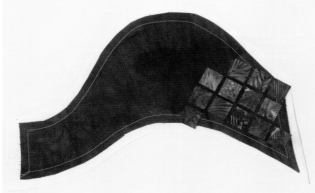

Begin in one corner.

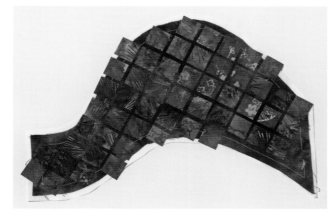

Fill in area.

Mosaics—Strips

Narrow strips can be appliquéd to a background segment at regular or irregular intervals. Apply paper-backed fusible web to the back of the strip fabric, then peel off the backing paper. Use a rotary cutter to cut strips at your chosen width and length, then position them on the segment fabric background. Press in place.

Fuse strips across segment, and stitch.

Consider stitching these in position using one or more of those decorative stitches programmed into your sewing machine.

Mosaics—Irregular Tiles

Another option is to create your own unique shapes that work well inside the segment outline. Prepare the background following the information given on pages 36–37, Steps 1–3.

1. Draw your mosaic design on the freezer paper, and remove it from the background fabric. Number each tile so you can reposition the tiles in the correct order later.

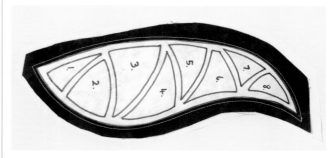

Draw design on freezer paper guide.

2. Cut a piece of paper-backed fusible web slightly larger than the freezer paper shape, and iron it to the back of the selected tile fabric.

3. Press the freezer paper guide to the right side of the fabric, making sure it lines up with the paper-backed fusible web on the back.

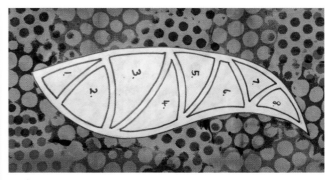

Iron freezer paper guide to front of fabric.

4. Cut out each tile, using the freezer paper as a guide. Position the tiles on the fabric background, staying inside the stitched outline. Remove the freezer paper and the paper backing from each tile, and press in place.

For larger segments, trace the original design onto a piece of clear plastic or tracing paper before the freezer paper is cut up. Lay this guide over the fabric background segment, and carefully line up the tiles in their corresponding places.

Leave freezer paper on surface of each tile until it is placed in position.

Position tiles on background, and press.

For some fabrics, it may be more effective to cut up the freezer paper guide and position the parts on different areas of the fabric to get a greater range of color gradation.

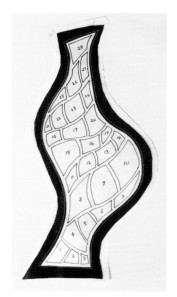

Draw design on freezer paper.

Cut up pattern, and position pieces in different places.

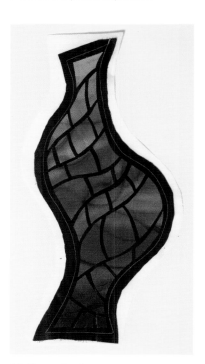

All tiles are in place.

Experiment with shapes within the confines of the outline. Try starting with a circle, and then work out with complementary adjoining shapes.

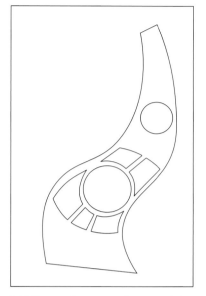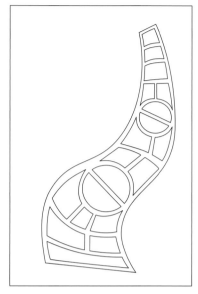

Initially two circles were drawn, and then extra shapes were added.

Mosaics—Stitching Tiles

After all the tiles are in place, anchor each tile with stitching. Generally, straight, satin, blanket, or triple stitching are the preferred options. There are, of course, many stitches that are suitable, so take time to explore some of those possibilities on your machine. Refer to the stitching techniques outlined on pages 66–75.

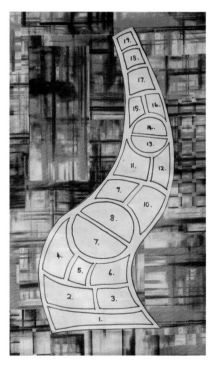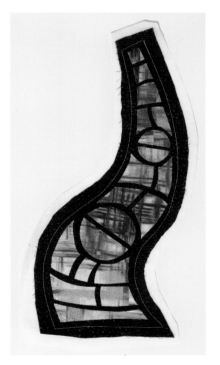

Multicolored fabrics provide variation.

Changes in color and shape are effective.

Piecing

Small squares, diamonds, or strips can be pieced together to create an area of fabric that can then be cut out to make a segment.

SQUARES

1. Draw the squares on the freezer paper pattern for this segment. Place the squares on point rather than vertically to let the colors wash across the surface.

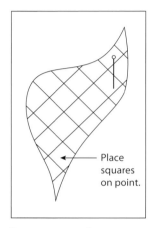

Draw squares on freezer paper.

2. Rotary cut the squares from selected fabrics, adding an extra ½″ (1.3cm) for seam allowances. For example, if the finished square size is to be 1½″ × 1½″ (3.8cm × 3.8cm), cut the squares 2″ × 2″ (5.1cm × 5.1cm).

3. Arrange these squares on the freezer paper pattern, overlapping the drawn squares and overlapping the segment pattern outline by at least ½″ (1.3cm). You can wash the colors across the surface, gradually changing the hue, or completely mix up the colors and values.

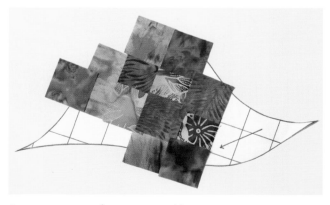

Arrange squares on freezer paper guide.

Add squares until segment is covered.

4. Once the squares have been covered and you are happy with the arrangement of colors and patterns, sew the squares together to make diagonal rows.

5. Press the rows in opposite directions, and then sew the rows together, nesting the seams. Follow the freezer paper pattern so the pieced fabric will cover the segment as planned.

6. Press the freezer paper pattern on the right side, aligning the drawn lines with the seams.

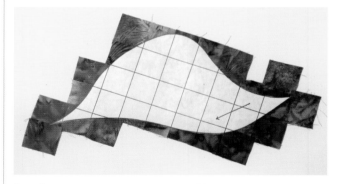

Press freezer paper pattern on top, matching squares.

7. Place this unit on tear-away stabilizer, and stitch around the edge of the freezer paper pattern ⅛″ (3mm) out from the edge. Trim the seam allowance to ½″ (1.3cm).

Finished segment

DIAMONDS

Follow the steps outlined for squares (page 56), replacing the segment squares with diamonds. To draw the diamonds on the freezer paper pattern, follow the steps outlined on pages 50–51, substituting freezer paper for the fusible web.

Another alternative is to cut the diamonds from fabric strips using a rotary cutter and the 30° line on your ruler, using the dimensions shown in the following illustration and the accompanying chart. For example, for a finished **B** distance of 2″ (5.1cm) wide, start with a fabric strip with an **A** distance of 2½″ (6.4cm) wide. To cut a diamond, line up the ruler's 30° line with the bottom of the strip, cut the strip across at this 30° angle, and then cut another parallel line across the strip 2½″ (6.4cm) away. Continue cutting parallel lines 2½″ (6.4cm) apart to cut multiple diamond shapes.

A third method is to cut around individual diamond stencils that are available in multiple sizes. These are very useful if you are cutting just one or two shapes from many different fabrics.

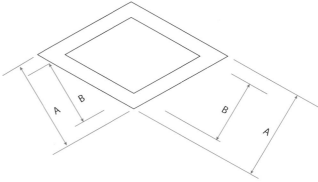

Diamonds can be cut any size.

CUT STRIP	CUT DIAMOND	FINISHED DIAMOND
Fabric strip width	Distance between parallel edges (A)*	Distance between parallel edges (B)
1¼″ (3.1cm)	1¼″ (3.1cm)	¾″ (1.9cm)
1⅜″ (3.5cm)	1⅜″ (3.5cm)	⅞″ (2.2cm)
1⅝″ (4.1cm)	1⅝″ (4.1cm)	1⅛″ (2.9cm)
1⅞″ (4.8cm)	1⅞″ (4.8cm)	1⅜″ (3.5cm)
2⅛″ (5.4cm)	2⅛″ (5.4cm)	1⅝″ (4.1cm)
2¼″ (5.7cm)	2¼″ (5.7cm)	1¾″ (4.4cm)
2½″ (6.4cm)	2½″ (6.4cm)	2″ (5.1cm)
2¾″ (7cm)	2¾″ (7cm)	2¼″ (5.7cm)

Includes ¼″ (7mm) seam allowance all around

Pieced diamond segments create interest.

FOUNDATION PIECING

To accurately join pieces for the background segment using the foundation piecing method, follow these steps.

1. Trace the outline of a segment onto a piece of tear-away stabilizer. Include all the piecing lines. Cut it out with an extra ½″ (1.3cm) border around the edge of the drawn line.

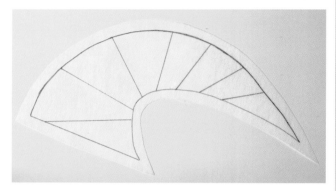

Trace outline onto tear-away stabilizer.

2. Turn it over and trace the outline through to the back. Draw a dotted line over the piecing lines. Write the word "back" on this side to avoid confusion later on when positioning the fabric.

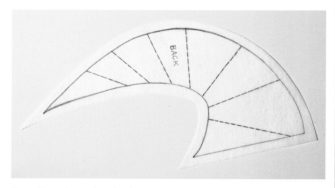

Trace lines through to back.

3. Turn the tear-away stabilizer so the front side is facing up. Select fabric for the first wedge, and cut it out, fully covering the drawn wedge and adding a ½″ seam allowance all around.

4. Place Wedge 1 in position with its right side up on the tear-away stabilizer, making sure the seam allowance overlaps the drawn wedge all around on the tear-away stabilizer.

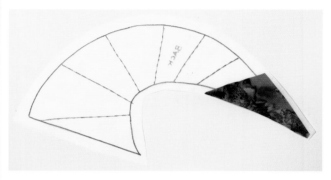

Place first wedge in position on tear-away stabilizer.

5. Similarly, cut out Wedge 2. Position Wedge 2 in place, matching adjoining edges, right sides together. Check that when the fabric wedge is flipped over, the drawn wedge on the tear-away stabilizer is covered.

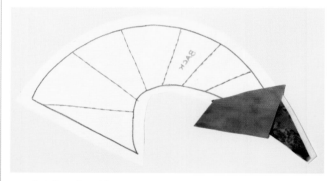

Match right sides of first two wedges.

6. With the back side of the stabilizer facing up, stitch on the dotted line, starting a couple of stitches before the line begins and continuing on for 2 stitches at the end of the line.

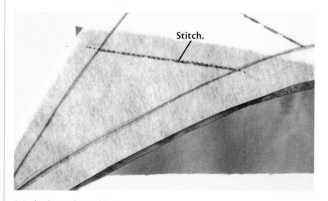

Stitch along dotted line.

7. Turn the tear-away stabilizer so the right side is facing up, flip over the second wedge, and finger-press or iron in position.

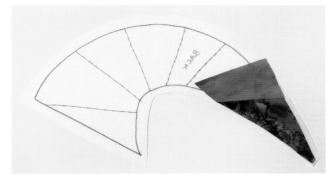

Flip over second wedge.

8. After each wedge is stitched in position, finger-press the side of the fabric covering the next edge back on the line to create a fold line in the fabric. Cut the seam allowance back to ¼" (7mm). Use this fold line as a guide when positioning the next wedge.

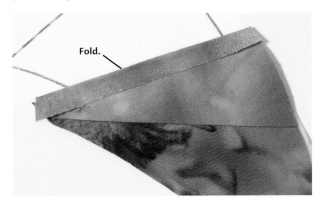

Finger-press fabric back along fold line.

9. Keep adding adjacent wedges in the same manner until all are in place.

Add wedges until complete.

10. Turn the tear-away stabilizer over so the back is facing up, and stitch a line of straight stitching ⅛" (3mm) out from the outside drawn line on the tear-away stabilizer. Trim the extra fabric on the outside edges back to a ½" (1.3cm) seam allowance where necessary.

Feature Fabrics

There are some fabrics that are so beautiful you can't imagine cutting them up. These fabrics can be featured without any further decoration. There will also be some segments that should not be decorated so that there is contrast and the overall design is not lost due to overdecoration.

These undecorated segments can be cut out using the freezer paper patterns as a guide. Iron the freezer paper to the right side of the fabric, and cut out with a ½" (1.3cm) seam allowance. Stitch a row of straight stitching ⅛" (3mm) out from the freezer paper edge. The layer of tear-away stabilizer is not necessary, but I sometimes still add this layer before stay stitching if the fabric is fragile or slippery.

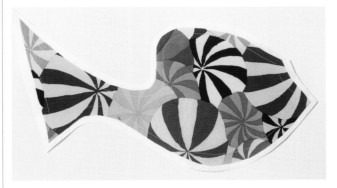

Beautifully patterned fabrics don't need further decoration.

Beading and Braids

The surface of the quilt can be further enhanced with the addition of beading or braids. Try using hand-dyed rick-rack or other sumptuous braids available on the market. They can be placed along an edge or used to decorate segments.

When using braid along an edge, use the stay-stitched guide to assist you in placement. When the adjacent segment is appliquéd in place, the braid will be partially hidden and will be secure.

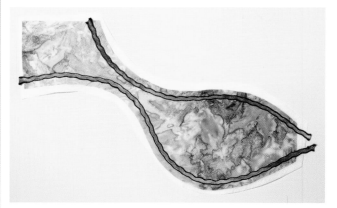

Stitch braid along edges of segment.

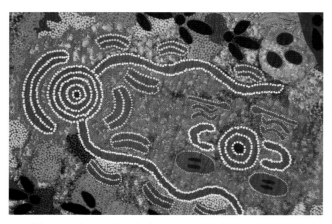

Detail from *Karkarooc* by Olinda Poulton. Use beads to decorate segments.

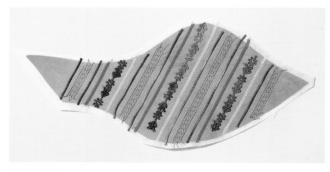

Stitch braids across a segment.

Detail of rickrack inserted into seam allowance in *Playing on the Surface* (quilt on page 88)

EARTH STRATA, 15½" × 22" (39cm × 56cm), Gloria Loughman

Although there are so many beautiful fabrics available for textile artists today, there is nothing like creating your own. Painting allows you to create a unique piece of fabric with your chosen colors in the right places. Consider painting your fabric to allow you the color changes or patterns you are trying to achieve.

Preparing to Paint

FABRIC PAINT

There are quite a few different fabric paints on the market. I live in Australia, so the one I find the cheapest and easiest to use is Hi Strike, sold by Batik Oetoro in New South Wales. In the United States, Setacolor is the fabric paint of choice, and Silhouette is popular in New Zealand. All are transparent paints and leave the fabric feeling soft. They can be diluted considerably for colorwashes and work well on cotton or silk. They are permanent when dried and ironed.

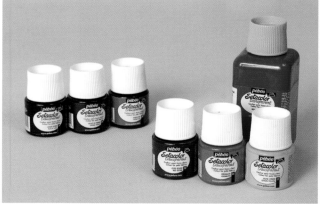

Fabric paints and brushes

BRUSHES

Sponge brushes are inexpensive and excellent tools, as they absorb a large quantity of paint and are very easy to use. They come in various widths with a blade-shaped foam head. They can be used to apply a smooth wide layer of paint or, using the sharp edge, a fine narrow line.

Regular brushes also come in a range of sizes and types. As most of the paint is applied with a sponge brush, you need just a few brushes for special effects. They might include stencil, fan, square, and pointed brushes. The key to selecting brushes is that you need them to be large enough to hold an adequate amount of paint.

FABRIC

White cotton fabric is an excellent choice for fabric painting; although, in reality, any fabric can be painted. White as a starting point gives you very accurate finished colors in comparison to beige or cream. You don't need to prewash the fabric before you paint unless it has a finish that prevents the paint from being absorbed.

PAINTING BOARDS

Lightweight foamcore boards (covered with plastic) or white melamine boards are excellent flat surfaces to spread fabric on. These can be positioned on a table for painting, and then situated in a sunny spot on the lawn or deck while the fabric dries. Alternatively, you can spread out sheets of plastic, or you may even be tempted to paint fabric directly on a tabletop. The paint will easily wash off solid surfaces. Be aware of what is under the fabric as it is drying, because a crease in the plastic will probably result in a white line on the fabric. Likewise, don't put fabric on paving stones to dry, as you will be certain to get a paving pattern on the fabric.

Applying the Paint

1. Dilute the paint, mixing approximately 2 parts water to 1 part paint. This will vary depending on the depth of the color you want to use.

2. Moisten the fabric by submerging it in a container of water. Stretch the fabric onto a solid, nonporous surface (such as one of those mentioned above), easing out air bubbles and removing loose threads. (Note: These threads can create wonderful lines if left on the fabric, because their white image is left behind when they are removed at the end of the drying process.)

3. Apply the diluted color with foam brushes. Dabbing creates texture while long brush strokes produce smooth color. Begin with the lightest colors first, laying down a basic wash of paint, blending the colors. You can always go darker, but sometimes it is difficult when using transparent paint to go lighter. Then it is time to go back over areas, creating highlights and contrasts.

Begin with lightest colors first, laying down a basic wash.

4. Apply details with a fine brush.

5. After you have finished painting, place the stretched fabric in the sun to dry.

6. After the fabric is dry, remove it from its base and iron it for 2 minutes on the reverse side. Try to allow at least 48 hours after ironing before washing by hand in warm water. After washing, air dry, and press the fabric so it is ready to use.

COASTAL STRATA, 17″ × 23″ (43cm × 58cm), Gloria Loughman

Detail of *Coastal Strata*

Gradations of Color

Beautiful pieces of fabric with gradual color changes can easily be created for mosaic work. Gradually add colors, overlapping to create beautiful mixes.

Graduate colors, overlapping to create more colors.

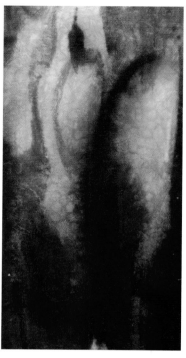

Use water spray to get colors to run.

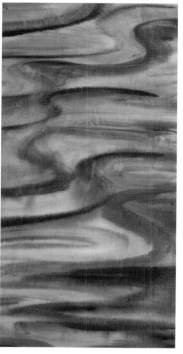

Swirl yellows and violet to create browns.

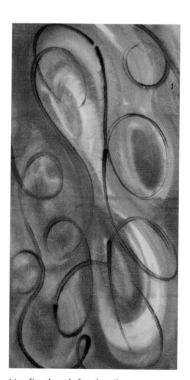

Use fine brush for detail.

Repeat patterns.

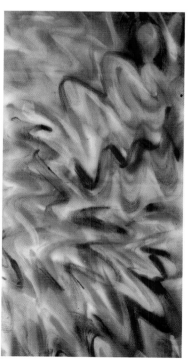

Use softer tones.

Sun Printing

The properties of transparent fabric paint make them suitable for helio-graphic fabric art, also known as sun printing. This very simple process allows you to create images on the fabric. Place items such as leaves, mesh, cardboard shapes, shells, lace, buttons, feathers, netting, and flowers on the surface of the fabric after you have applied the paint and it is still wet. When the fabric is dry, remove the objects and their image will remain. It is interesting that the area under the object dries lighter than the rest rather than darker.

Creating Textured Fabrics

You can create very interesting textures by scrunching or creasing wet, painted fabric and allowing it to dry on your board. Be sure to allow extra drying time.

Fabric created using leaves

ANCIENT WATER COURSE, 38″ × 55″ (96cm × 140cm), Gloria Loughman

The stitches presented in this chapter have been divided into stitches for appliquéing shapes fused to the base fabric and stitches for drawing and decoration. Most of the stitches outlined can be used for both purposes, so take that into account when looking for ideas.

Appliqué Stitching Options

Satin stitching completely encloses the raw edge and has a crisp, stable finish that provides a well-defined image. In contrast, raw-edge appliqué involves free-motion (straight) stitching around the motif edge to capture the threads and tends to be more subtle and understated. Decide which is the most appropriate for your motif or edge.

Satin and free-motion stitching

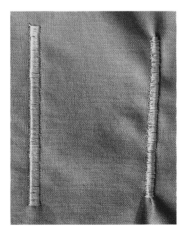

Stitching on left is stabilized; stitching on right is not stabilized and puckers.

SATIN-STITCH APPLIQUÉ

Satin stitching uses the zigzag stitch with the stitch length set very short so that the stitches sit snugly against each other. The tear-away stabilizer is already in place on the back of the segment, so the base fabric is stabilized. Unstabilized fabric will pucker, and the quality of the satin stitch will not be good.

Preparation

1. Prepare the fabric pieces to be stitched following the instructions in Appliqué Motifs—Regular Shapes (page 44) using paper-backed fusible web.

2. Choose a needle that is appropriate for the thread size (see table). Ideally, you want the smallest needle possible, because a satin stitch creates 2 parallel lines of tiny holes, very close to each other, which need to be filled with thread.

THREAD SIZE	NEEDLE SIZE
60	60/8
50	70/10
40	80/12
30/35	90/14
20/12	100/16

3. Use a foot that allows you to see where you are going. The open-toe appliqué foot is my preferred option; or use a clear plastic foot that allows you to see your work as you stitch.

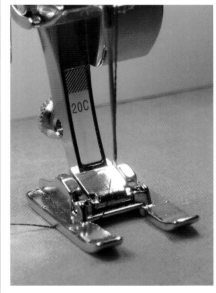

Open-toe appliqué foot

4. Select the zigzag setting, and adjust the stitch width to approximately 2. This width setting will vary, of course, depending on the sewing machine and the size of the motif being appliquéd. For a large motif it would probably be more appropriate to use a wider stitch of perhaps 3 or more. For tiny pieces, a stitch width of 1 would be more suitable, but remember your glasses!

5. Thread your machine with a thread color that matches or contrasts with the motif color. Rayon or polyester machine embroidery thread in 40-weight are both excellent threads for satin stitch, as they seem to sit flatter than some of the other threads available.

6. Make sure that the bobbin thread is wound smoothly and evenly. You can use a fine special-purpose bobbin thread or a polyester thread in a similar color to the top thread. Don't try to save money by using a cheaper-quality thread on the bobbin. It is likely to cause you all kinds of problems, as these threads tend to be uneven and quite thick. For satin stitching, it is preferable to have a bobbin thread equal in weight or finer than the top thread.

7. You will need a fairly tight bobbin tension and a slightly loosened top tension. Check the bobbin tension first to make sure that it is firm and not too loose. If you are using a Bernina sewing machine, thread the bobbin thread through the finger on the bobbin case to further tighten the bobbin tension. Adjust the top tension down to a lower number—for example, from 5 to 3. Practice on a sample of fabric backed with tear-away stabilizer.

To achieve a perfect satin stitch, the top thread should be pulled down to the underside. On the underside of your work, the top thread should appear like a railway line on either side of the bobbin thread. If the top thread is not visible, or if any of the bobbin thread is showing on the top, turn the top tension dial down further, and try again. When changing threads, you will need to recheck the tension by stitching on the sample.

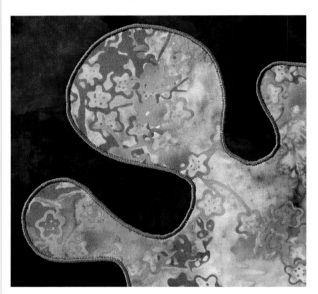

Practice on sample.

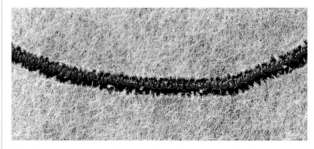

Good tension—turquoise top thread appears on back on both sides of orange bobbin thread.

> **tip** When practicing, use scraps of the same motif fabric so you can check the color of the thread as well as the tension.

Adjusting the Bobbin Tension

Think of the bobbin tension screw as the face of a clock. Turn it to the right (clockwise) to tighten. Turn it to the left (counterclockwise) to loosen. Be sure to move it in tiny increments when adjusting—five minutes at a time.

Adjusting bobbin tension

If your machine has a drop-in bobbin, you can still adjust the tension using the tension screw that is usually situated in the center front of the bobbin housing. The same rules apply: turn it to the right to tighten, and to the left to loosen.

8. The final adjustment is the stitch length. This should be quite small but with enough length that when you let go of the fabric, the feed dogs will still carry it through. You are aiming to have the stitches as close together as possible, but the work will still move freely through the machine without being pushed. The length will probably be set in the vicinity of 0.25 to 0.5. The stitch width and length should be checked on the sample before you set to work on the real thing. Although initially this testing takes time, in the long run you save hours of frustration, as unpicking stitches is time consuming and poor workmanship is disappointing.

Aim to have stitches close together.

Stitching

1. Start stitching on a straight section, as it is easier to get a feel for where you are heading, and you can disguise the start and finish points more easily. When you start, bring the bobbin thread up to the top of your work, and then proceed to stitch around the motif. The stitches should rest mainly on the piece being appliquéd. Keep the stitches at 90° to the edge of the motif by turning the work slowly and evenly. Try to keep sewing longer runs, gradually rotating your work rather than starting and stopping.

2. When you reach the point when you need to change the angle to go around a steeper curve, stop your machine with the needle down on the outside of the curve. Lift the foot, turn the fabric slightly, and lower the foot to sew a few more stitches. Continue in this way—sewing, stopping, pivoting, sewing, and so on—until the curve is completed. If you stop on the inside of a curve and pivot, you will get small gaps in the stitching.

3. If you need to sew around a corner or point, you have a couple of alternatives. For wide corners, stitch right to the end, reposition the needle, and then proceed in the new direction. For narrow points, gradually decrease the stitch width as you approach the point, stop with the needle down, swing your work around, and then increase the width and stitch in the new direction.

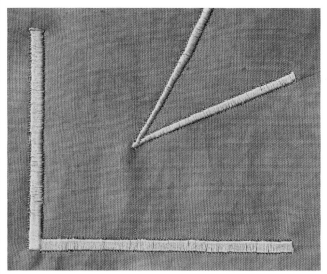

Satin stitch around wide and narrow corners

4. When you have returned to the starting point, overlap 2 or 3 stitches. Tie off the threads at the back of the work to finish. If you are stopping at the edge of another fabric, stitch 3 or 4 stitches into the next fabric, and stop. Tie off the threads on the back. When you stitch the next fabric, these stitches will be covered.

Detail of narrow satin stitch around free-flowing shapes from *Kimberley Mystique* (quilt on page 4)

SOFT- OR RAW-EDGE APPLIQUÉ

Another method for securing fused motifs is to free-motion stitch around the outer edge. This is often the preferred option for those edges that are complex and difficult to sew around with conventional stitches. Using a darning foot, free-motion stitching requires you to drop or cover the feed dogs, and then you can move the fabric in any direction. Mastering this technique opens up a whole new world of stitching possibilities, not just for appliqué but for machine embroidery as well.

Darning foot

Preparation

1. Set up a practice sample of fabric pinned to a piece of tear-away stabilizer.

2. Attach the darning foot, consulting the machine manual if you haven't done this before.

3. Drop or cover the feed dogs, and release the presser foot if necessary.

4. Adjust the stitch width to zero.

5. For free-motion stitching, you need a fairly tight bobbin tension and a slightly loosened top tension. Adjust the top tension down 1 or 2 numbers. If the normal top tension is 5, try 3 for free-motion stitching. If you can still see the bobbin thread coming through to the top, further reduce the top tension until it disappears. If you have reduced the top tension to zero and you can still see the bobbin thread coming through to the top, then you need to tighten the bobbin case underneath (page 69).

Practice drawing and free-motion stitching around motifs.

Stitching

1. Place the fabric backed with tear-away stabilizer under the darning foot, and lower the foot.

2. Lower the needle into the work, and gently press on the foot pedal while steadily moving the fabric. Just think of the needle as a pencil that is fixed into position, and you are moving the paper underneath it to draw a pattern. When you first try this technique it feels quite different, and you crave more control. Once you have mastered it, though, it is the most liberating and exciting technique.

3. Try drawing a few circles; then draw some flowers or leaves. Try tracing around some of the patterns on the fabric, and then echo stitch a number of times.

Have fun drawing with thread around patterns in fabric.

4. Once you feel reasonably confident, try stitching around fused shapes. Thread your machine with a thread that is as close as possible in color to the motif fabric. The bobbin thread can be matching or neutral in color. As you become more experienced, try using contrasting-colored threads.

5. Place the fabric with the fused motif, backed with tear-away stabilizer, under the darning foot, then lower the presser foot.

6. Lower the needle into the work, close to the edge of the motif, and take one stitch, ending with the needle up.

7. Pull the top thread to bring up the bobbin thread. If possible, set the needle position to down.

8. Start stitching, gently moving the fabric, trying to get the stitches even. Proceed around the outside edge of the motif.

9. Secure the ends, tying them off on the back.

Try to stitch ⅟₁₆″ (2mm) from fused edge.

You will find that some fabrics fray more than others. Batiks, which have a very high thread count, are less likely to fray than a more open-weave fabric. You can add a second row of stitching during the quilting process to help prevent fraying.

Finding Your Free-Motion Speed

Remember that you are in control of moving the fabric, as you have taken on the role of the feed dogs. If you move it very slowly, you will get tiny stitches. If you move it quickly, you will get large stitches. If you don't move it at all, you will get a buildup of stitches on one spot. There must be a balance between the stitching speed of the machine, maintained by your pressure on the foot pedal, and the speed at which you move the fabric. Some people prefer to run the machine and move the fabric at high speed. Others proceed very slowly, even setting their machine to a lower speed if that is an option. Everyone has his or her own optimum speed that provides the greatest control. Personally, I am one of the slower, more cautious stitchers. With lots of practice you will settle into a rhythm that gives you the best results and affords you greater control.

PROGRAMMED STITCHES

There are quite a few stitches that are programmed into machines these days that can be used for appliqué. If you are like me and usually stick to straight and zigzag stitching, now it is time to experiment with the other 753-plus stitches available. Be adventurous, and try some of these around the outside edge of a fused motif or along the side of an edge treatment.

Programmed stitches add interest.

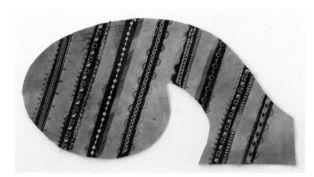

There are many programmed stitches to try.

Triple Stitch

A stitch that I find very effective both for appliqué and for stitching bold lines is the triple stitch. Many machines have this stitch, which is often made up of four stitches forward, two back, four forward, and so on. On more recent machines it has been programmed in at two stitches forward, one back, two forward. It effectively goes over the stitch three times, creating quite a strong line, especially if you use a 30-weight or thicker thread.

The symbol for the triple stitch on most machines is |||

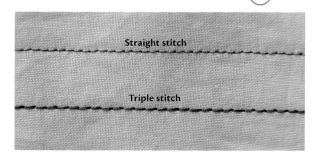

Contrast between straight and triple stitches

Triple stitch around mosaic shapes

Blanket Stitch

Although often used to create a country feel for quilts, the blanket stitch is a good option for appliqué, especially for sewing around small circular shapes. The double blanket stitch, an additional stitch on more recent machines, provides for an almost lacy finish when used around the edges of small shapes. It looks bolder than the single stitch because another stitch is sewn on top of the first one.

Double blanket stitch gives lacy edge.

Decorative Stitching Options

FREE-MOTION STITCHING

If you haven't tried this technique before—or have, and felt "all at sea"—read through the section on raw-edge appliqué (pages 70–71), which details setting up your machine for free-motion stitching. Instead of stitching around the edge of a motif, it is now time to doodle. Time to draw and create patterns—the scribbles you would normally do with a pencil to create a design.

Practice on a sample first before you stitch on the segments.

1. Place some tear-away stabilizer under the practice area to be embellished, and thread your machine. The top thread can be any weight from 12- to 50-weight. I prefer 30- or 40-weight thread for most of my embellishing, as it is easy to manage and is thick enough to build up quickly and be noticed. On the bobbin you have a choice of one of the finer bobbin threads or a thread that matches the top thread in color and weight. Check the table on page 67 for the appropriate needle type and size.

Practice on sample backed with tear-away stabilizer.

2. There are numerous ways that you can hold your work to get as much control as possible as you free-motion stitch. I usually hold the work flat, with my left hand on the top, and move the fabric with my right hand holding on underneath. Some quilters prefer to place both hands on the top of the work, and others use aides such as gloves to assist in the manipulation of the fabric. Just as machine stitching speed is a personal preference, you will also find that with practice you will develop your own comfortable position for holding your work as you move it under the needle.

3. Place the fabric backed with tear-away stabilizer under the darning foot, and lower the presser foot and then the needle into the work. The needle-down position should be engaged.

4. Gradually move the fabric while stitching, trying to keep the stitches even. Without turning the fabric, stitch while moving it forward, backward, and sideways. Try small circles and spirals. The faster you move the fabric, the longer the stitches; the slower you move, the shorter the stitches. It takes a while to get even stitches, but practice develops the ability to stitch in any direction, creating fluid lines. Having your machine in needle-down mode prevents your work from moving while you stop to catch your breath.

5. When you are finished, secure the ends by tying them together on the back of your work.

EMBELLISHING WITH THICKER THREADS

There are some threads that are fun to use but far too thick to pass through the needle and the tension on the top of the sewing machine. These threads can easily be wound onto a bobbin, either manually or using the bobbin winding mechanism on your machine.

Of course, when this embellishing thread is on the bobbin, it must be sewn with the back of the work facing up. Try drawing your design onto the tear-away stabilizer on the back of the segment, and then use it as a guide.

Experiment with thicker threads.

1. Before sewing with the thicker thread, check the bobbin tension. Pull out a short length of the thread from the bobbin case to make sure it slides out smoothly. As you are using a thicker thread than normal, it will probably feel too tight. Loosen the screw on the bobbin case by turning it to the left about 10 minutes on the clock face. Recheck by pulling out more of the thread until it glides out smoothly, without too much drag. If you enjoy stitching with thicker threads, purchase another bobbin case and have it permanently set on a looser setting. Label this extra bobbin case so that it is easily discernable from your regular case. There are some machines, especially those with drop-in bobbin cases, that allow you to bypass the bobbin tension altogether. Place the bobbin in the bobbin case, and then draw up the bobbin thread through the machine plate, ready to start stitching. Don't thread it through the narrow tension slot first; just leave it loose.

2. Select a regular-weight top thread in a color that matches the thicker bobbin thread.

3. Change the top tension to a higher number or setting than normal, such as 6 or 7 or +.

4. Free-motion stitch from the back of your work, creating closely stitched textures or free-flowing lines. I would suggest that you use 2 layers of tear-away stabilizer, sew at a slower speed, and make the stitches a little larger to show off the beautiful threads.

5. To finish, pull the threads to the back of your work and tie them off.

DRAWING LINES WITH THREAD

For strong drawn lines, try satin stitch (page 67), triple stitch (page 72), and many of the other programmed stitches on your machine.

Strong drawn lines using straight and programmed stitches

Satin-stitched line divides segment.

COMBINATIONS OF STITCHING TECHNIQUES

Consider outlining a shape with a bold stitching line such as triple stitch, then fill in the outline with a web of lines, small circles, meanders, or other shapes. It is sometimes useful to cut out the shape you want to draw from freezer paper, and iron this in place. This will provide a guide so that the outline stitching is accurate.

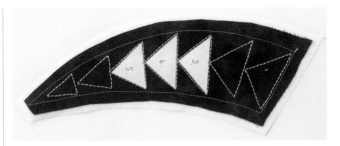

Outline freezer paper guides in triple stitch.

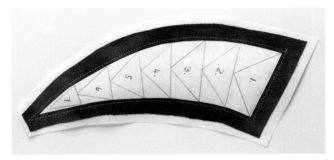

Background segment with freezer paper still attached

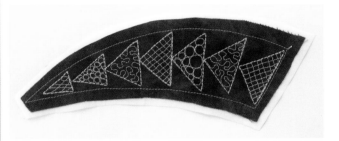

Three options for filling in with free-motion machine stitching

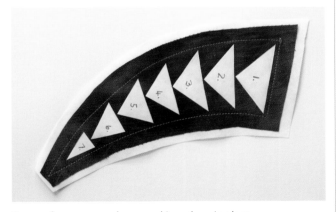

Cut out freezer paper shapes and iron them in place.

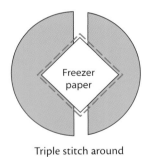

Freezer paper

Triple stitch around freezer paper guide.

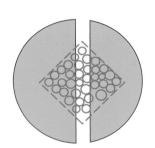

Remove freezer paper and stitch small circles inside square.

Examples of decorative stitching from *Kimberley Mystique* (quilt on page 4)

KARIJINI GORGES AND GUMTREES,
24″ × 34″ (61cm × 86.4cm), Janet Greeks

Curved edge binding provides effective edge treatment.

OCTOPUS GARDEN, 33″ × 28″ (84cm × 72cm), Merrilyn Crabbe

Narrow inner border gives extra definition to this quilt.

Details from *Sunflowers at Cave Springs* (quilt on page 81).
Design extends out into border on this quilt.

MEANDERING, 16″ × 27¼″ (40.6cm × 69.2cm), Bonny Voice
Faced edges make this quilt possible.

Photo by April Wegren

Borders

Borders can create a sense of completion and can make an image appear larger and bolder. But be careful—unsuitable borders can really detract.

A frame that is a similar color will extend your work, with the design flowing visually out into the border. One that is contrasting will make the work seem smaller by defining the edges of the work itself.

Audition a range of light and dark fabrics. You will find that a dark border around a dark work will make the lighter areas stand out. Conversely, a light border around a light work will tend to highlight the darker areas. A border that matches the color on one side of the quilt top and contrasts with the other side can also be quite effective.

Sometimes a border can confine a quilt too much, so consider just applying a binding or facing and having no borders at all.

There are some designs that just call out for the corners to be mitered, while others are quite pleasing to the eye with square corners.

Select the borders to bring out the best in your work. Pin the quilt top to your design wall and try different-colored fabrics around the edge. Try different widths and combinations. Stand back and decide which one looks best. Remember, the borders should complement the design and not distract the viewer from the main composition.

NARROW INNER BORDERS

Picture framers often use a narrow inside border before adding the large outside mat. The purpose of this inner border is to break up the movement of color flowing to the outer border. It is especially useful to break up areas of dark color in the composition that link to a dark border fabric.

You can replicate this effect in fabric by making a ¼" (7mm) or even a ⅛" (3mm) inside border. There is a simple procedure you can follow to ensure that the narrow frame is symmetrical and parallel.

1. Remove as much tear-away stabilizer as possible from the back of the quilt top without putting too much stress on the stitches.

2. Square up the quilt top using a large cutting mat and ruler to ensure accuracy. A large 12½" (31.7cm) square ruler is very useful for this purpose.

Square up the quilt top with rulers and a cutting mat.

3. Cut 2 strips 1¼" (3.1cm) wide for the narrow side borders. This is wider than necessary, but the extra width helps prevent stretching when the borders are applied. Trim the narrow side borders the same length as the measurement through the center of the quilt top. Piece the borders if necessary to achieve the correct length (page 82).

Make borders same length as measurement through center of quilt.

4. Pin and stitch these narrow side borders in place, using an accurate ¼″ (7mm) seam allowance. Press them toward the outside edge.

5. Cut strips 1¼″ (3.1cm) wide for the top and bottom narrow borders. Trim the narrow top and bottom borders the same length as the measurement through the center of the quilt top, including the side borders. Piece the borders if necessary. Pin and stitch the narrow top and bottom borders in place, using an accurate ¼″ (7mm) seam allowance. Press them toward the outside edge.

6. Cut side outer border pieces to the desired width plus 1″ (2.5cm). Trim the side borders the same length as the measurement through the center of the quilt top, including the narrow inner borders. Piece these outer borders if necessary to achieve the correct length (page 82).

Make outer border same length as extended measurement across center.

7. Attach the side outer border to the edge of the first narrow border, matching long edges, with right sides together. Turn the quilt top over so that the outer side border is now on the bottom. Sew the seam from this side, lining up the left side of the ¼″ (7mm) foot with the previous stitching line. To create an even smaller narrow border, line up the left inside edge of the foot with the initial stitching line, or move the needle position to the left. The distance between the first stitching line and this second row of stitching is the finished width of the narrow inside border.

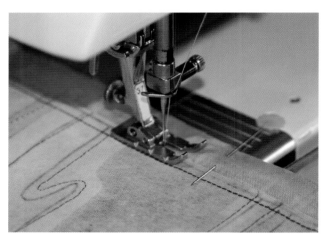

Line up edge of ¼″ (7mm) foot with the first stitching line.

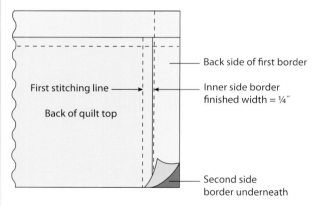

Distance between stitching lines is finished width of narrow inside border.

8. Trim the seam allowance back to ¼″ (7mm), and press.

9. Attach the other side outer border, then cut and attach the top and bottom outer borders in the same way.

Narrow border followed by wider outer border allows extra space for quilting.

> **tip** Always stitch the side borders before the top and bottom borders so that there are no distracting vertical lines heading off the top and bottom edges of the quilt.

Quilting

The quilting process allows you to further enhance your design. Be inspired by the shapes and textures that you have already created. For example, if spirals have been appliquéd in a panel, quilted spirals will add harmony and complement the design. Patterns in the fabrics will also give you great ideas for quilting.

Quilted spirals next to appliquéd spirals on *Playing on the Surface* (quilt on page 42)

Echo quilting on *Surface Energy* (quilt on page 84)

Quilting picks up patterns in fabric and leaf theme on *Dappled Forest* (quilt on page 95).

Layer the backing fabric, batting, and quilt top, using masking tape to anchor each of the three layers to a flat surface. Stretch each layer slightly so there are no creases or wrinkles. Baste the three layers together with safety pins every 3"–4" (7.6cm–10cm).

When free-motion quilting, it is crucial that you get the tension setting correct. As both sides of your work will be on show, you need to have balanced, even stitches on the top and the bottom. Test your stitches and threads on a sample made up of the fabrics and batting you plan to use. Practice stitching the sample the way you intend to quilt your project. If you are quilting circles, stitch circles on the sample. Using the same color of thread on the top and bottom can help solve tension issues.

Machine quilt in the ditch around the main elements, using threads that match the fabrics as much as possible. Now have fun quilting each segment, echoing shapes or introducing new designs that complement the theme. The quilting lines will give more texture to the surface. You can match the color of the thread to the area you are quilting or use a contrasting thread for elements that you wish to accent. For more information on free-motion stitching techniques, see pages 73–75.

Bindings

Once again, color choice is crucial. On many quilts, the binding is the same color as the outside borders so as not to introduce another distraction. For other designs, the binding is the only frame and it needs to give some closure to the edge of the composition.

For most of my larger quilts, I try to create a frame that harmonizes with the surrounding areas of the quilt but still provides visual definition and support.

WIDE BINDING

1. If you are planning to use a wide binding, then before quilting cut the backing and batting 4" (10cm) larger than the quilt top. Sandwich the quilt with a 2" (5.1cm) edge of batting visible all around the quilt top. After quilting, square up the "quilt sandwich," as the edges may have

distorted slightly during the quilting process. Trim the backing and batting so there is 1½" (3.8cm) all around the proposed edge of the quilt top. It is very important to check the squareness of the quilt sandwich before applying the bindings.

2. Cut binding strips, 8½" (21.3cm) wide, crosswise from the binding fabric. Piece the binding strips as necessary to make the side, top, and bottom binding strips (see Joining Strips for Bindings, page 82).

3. Fold the strips in half lengthwise, with wrong sides together, and press.

4. Starting with the opposite side edges, pin the folded binding along the front edges of the quilt top, 1½" (3.8cm) in from the outside edges of the backing and binding. Stitch with an accurate ¼" (7mm) seam.

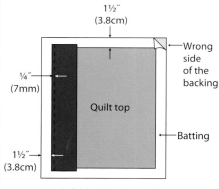

Stitch folded binding to front edge of quilt top.

5. Bring the folded edge of the binding strips to the back of the quilt, turning them around the edge of the batting and backing, and firmly hand stitch in place on the back of the quilt. At the corners, trim the excess binding even with the outside edges of the quilt.

6. Attach binding strips to the top and bottom edges of the quilt in the same way, leaving a short overlap at each end. Turn the folded edges to the back of the quilt; tuck in the ends to create a neat, firm corner; and hand stitch in place.

NARROW BINDING

Quilts with wide borders and smaller quilts require a much narrower binding. You can adjust the width of the strips accordingly.

1. For a very narrow binding, cut strips 2" to 2½" (5.1cm–6.3cm) wide. Piece strips as necessary to achieve the correct length. For a more generous binding, cut the strips 3½" (9cm) wide.

2. Square up the quilt sandwich, trimming the backing and batting even with the quilt top.

3. Fold the binding strips in half lengthwise, with wrong sides together, and press.

4. Starting with the sides, pin the folded binding along the front edges of the quilt top.

5. Stitch the bindings in place.

6. Turn the folded edges to the back of the quilt, and firmly hand stitch in place.

7. Repeat with the top and bottom edges, tucking in the ends to create neat corners.

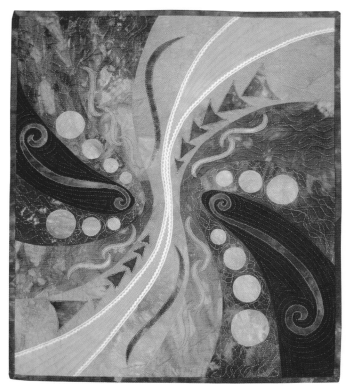

ENLIGHTENMENT, 20″ × 23″ (51cm × 59cm), Sonya Else

Narrow binding enhances this quilt.

SUNBAKED, 40½″ × 43¼″ (103cm × 110cm), Cheryl Anne Botha

Pattern continues into border. This quilt has a wide binding.

SUNFLOWERS AT CAVE SPRINGS, 39½″ × 32½″(100.3cm × 82.6cm), Lyn King

Another quilt with a wide binding

Joining Strips for Bindings

To make the joins less visible, sew the strips together on the diagonal.

Cut strips in your chosen widths and position two at right angles, right sides together. Stitch across the corner as shown. Trim the seam allowances, and press open.

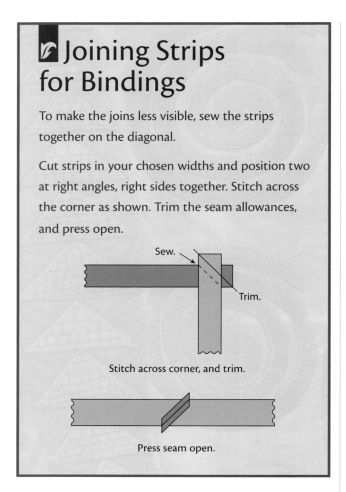

Stitch across corner, and trim.

Press seam open.

MITERED CORNERS

To miter binding corners, prepare the binding strip as outlined above (see Joining Strips for Bindings), creating a strip long enough to go around the quilt perimeter with at least 10″ (25.4cm) extra for mitering. For wide bindings, add additional length. Fold the strip in half lengthwise, wrong sides together, and press.

1. Attach the binding strip to the front side of the quilt sandwich, raw edges even, stopping ¼″ (7 mm) from the first corner, then backstitch.

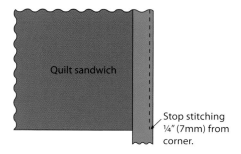

Stop stitching ¼″ (7mm) from corner.

2. Remove the quilt from under the foot and fold the binding up at a right angle.

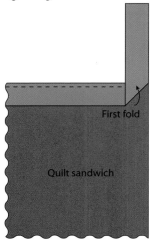

Fold binding up at right angle.

3. Fold the binding down again alongside the edge. Insert the needle ¼″ (7mm) from the corner, take a couple of stitches, then backstitch. Stitch to the next corner, and repeat the process.

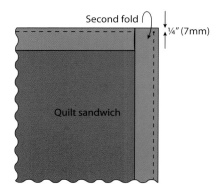

Fold down, and stitch to ¼″ (7mm) from corner.

4. When you return to the starting point, join the strips by overlapping them, folding the short edge of the ending tail to hide the raw end. Or, for a more elegant look, join them on the diagonal, as described on the C&T Publishing website. See Resources on page 103 for details.

5. After the binding is attached, bring the folded edge of the binding over the edges of the quilt sandwich, and pin to the back of the quilt. Use a matching-color thread to slipstitch the binding to the back of the quilt along the fold to cover the machine stitching.

FACED EDGE

For this technique it is extremely important to have the quilt sandwich as square and straight as possible.

1. Cut a strip 3″ (8cm) wide by the length of the side of the quilt (piece if necessary to achieve the correct length). With wrong sides together, press the strip in half lengthwise. Place the folded strip on a side edge of the quilt, with right sides together. Carefully align the raw edges, and pin in position. Sew the strip to the quilt with a ¼″ (7mm) seam allowance. If possible, use a walking or even-feed foot to keep an even pressure on the quilt sandwich.

Use walking foot to keep even pressure on quilt sandwich.

2. Press the facing out using a steam iron. Stitch a row of stay stitching ⅛″ (3mm) out from the seamline.

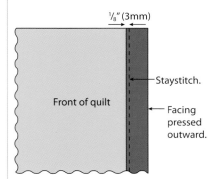

⅛″ (3mm)

Staystitch.

Front of quilt

Facing pressed outward.

Press facing out. Staystitch.

3. Fold the entire strip to the back of the quilt, and press to flatten the seam allowance. Slipstitch the folded edge to the back of the quilt.

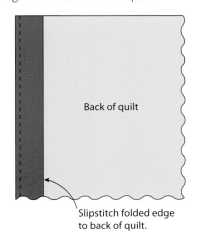

Back of quilt

Slipstitch folded edge to back of quilt.

Fold entire strip to back of quilt, and slipstitch.

4. Repeat this process on the opposite side of the quilt.

5. Repeat the process for the top and bottom facings, this time adding at least ½″ (1.3cm) on each end to fold to the back. Sew the facing to the quilt using a ¼″ (7mm) seam allowance. Don't forget to press flat and

staystitch. It may be necessary to trim the bulky seam allowance in the corner a little to get a flat finish.

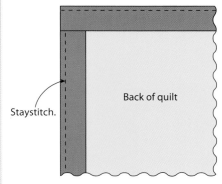

Back of quilt

Staystitch.

Fold under facing ends at corners, and slipstitch facing to back.

Faced edge of *Color Play* (quilt on page 92)

Finally, be sure to add a hanging sleeve to the back—made from fabric that matches the backing, if possible, for a professional look. Add a label with the relevant information.

SURFACE ENERGY, 18½″ × 32″ (48cm × 80cm), Melinda Gibson

OVER THE TOP, 43″ × 24″ (109cm × 61cm), Mary E. Williams

FIRE, 22¼″ × 31″ (56cm × 79cm), Linda O'Keefe

GECKO ON THE WIRE, 21″ × 30¼″ (53cm × 77cm), Elizabeth Fraser

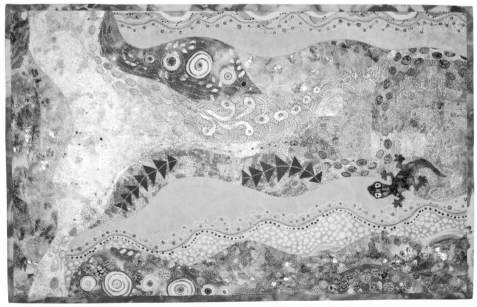

LAKE EYRE IN FLOOD, 15¾″ × 24½″ (40cm × 62cm), Caroline Sharkey

PEACOCK PASSION, 44″ × 35″ (112cm × 89cm), Pat Waller

Photo by Pat Waller

MOCK CHARGE, 25½″ × 32″ (64.5cm × 81cm), Jenny Waddell

REMEMBER SUMMER RAIN, 61″ × 30″ (155cm × 76cm), Debra Wight

EXPLOSION, 20¼″ × 24½″ (52cm × 62cm), Kellie Andersen

LEAVES, 29″ × 24″ (74cm × 61cm), Rhonda Atkinson

JEWELS OF THE OCEAN FLOOR, 35½″ × 23¼″ (90cm × 82cm),
Michelle Shane

ROCKY MOUNTAIN SUNRISE, 39″ × 27¾″ (99cm × 70.5cm), Jill Bell

Photo by J. S. Bell

RED DILEMMA, 25″ × 35″ (63.5cm × 89cm), Nola Williams

DANCE WITH ME HENRY, 26″ × 33″ (55cm × 84cm),
Helen Ward

Photo by Helen Ward

PLAYING ON THE SURFACE, 23″ × 31½″ (58cm × 80cm),
Leanne Beasley

Project 1:
Simple Appliqué and Foundation Piecing

CELEBRATION by Gloria Loughman

Finished size: 12″ × 16½″ (30cm × 42cm)

This small wallhanging is a great place to start when trying out surface techniques, including appliqué (page 43) and foundation piecing (pages 58–59).

Fabric Requirements

10–12 fabrics that vary in color, pattern, and value: ¼ yard (25cm) or a fat quarter of each for segments and inner border*

Backing: 14″ × 19″ (36cm × 48cm)

Binding: 8″ × 40″ (20cm × 102cm)

See Preparation (to the right) for further information on fabric choices.

Other Supplies

Freezer paper: 1 yard (1m)

Tear-away stabilizer: 1 yard (1m) of 40″ (102cm) wide tear-away or similar fabric stabilizer

Paper-backed fusible web: 1 yard (1m) of Wonder-Under, Steam-A-Seam, Vliesofix, or similar product

Batting: 14″ × 19″ (36cm × 48cm)

Invisible thread: nylon or polyester

Thread to match fabrics

Construction

PREPARATION

Use the project pattern from the pullout at the back of the book, and refer to pages 36–37 to create the tear-away stabilizer base, the freezer paper patterns, and the fabric backgrounds for Segments 1, 2, 4, 5, 7, and 8. Include the extra tear-away stabilizer layer, as these segments will be embellished (optional for Segment 8). Staystitch each segment fabric background piece, and remove the freezer paper. Note that in the sample, the same background fabric is used for Segments 1, 4, and 7 and another for Segments 2 and 5.

Prepare segment for embellishing.

EDGE TREATMENTS: SEGMENTS 1, 4, AND 7

Use the techniques outlined on pages 46–47 to complete these segments. When stitching appliqué shapes in place close to the edge, use the triple stitch for straight edges and the free-motion stitch for the small curved shapes.

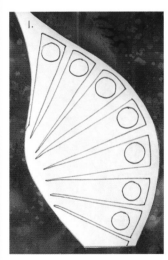

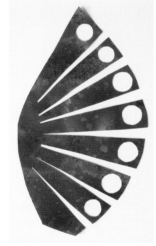

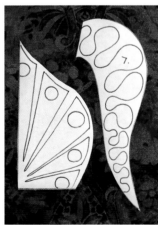

APPLIQUÉ: SEGMENTS 2 AND 5

The small circles for Segments 2 and 5 can be traced directly onto paper-backed fusible web, using a template or a thread spool as a guide. When stitching the shapes in place, use a straight stitch or another stitch of your choice. It is easiest to stitch around the circles using a darning foot and free-motion stitching techniques. Use the techniques on pages 70–71 for these segments.

FOUNDATION PIECING: SEGMENTS 3 AND 6

Trace the patterns for Segments 3 and 6 onto individual pieces of tear-away stabilizer (including the designs within the segments). Cut out the segment shapes slightly larger than the pattern outline. Following the directions on pages 58–59, foundation piece these sections. The fabrics used in the sample are graded from darker at the bottom to lighter at the top. After all areas have been covered, turn the segments over and straight stitch ⅛" (3mm) out from the drawn outline on the tear-away stabilizer.

SEGMENT 8

In the sample, Segment 8 is not embellished in any way. Your fabric choice will determine whether you need further decoration of this segment. If you do decide to add embellishment, remember to harmonize it with the rest of the design and add an extra layer of tear-away stabilizer. Perhaps a row of small circles or a repeat of the pattern in Segment 4 would be appropriate.

 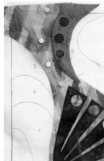

segments together, stitching them sequentially. Remember to clip the curves as needed.

Putting the Segments Together

Remove the tear-away stabilizer from the back of each segment. Refer to pages 37–41 to put all the

Finishing

Refer to Borders, Quilting, and Bindings (pages 76–83). Specific details for the sample project follow.

Trim the batting and backing to ½" (1.3cm) outside the quilt top. Cut strips 1" (2.5cm) wide for the narrow inner border. Place these border strips ⅝" (1.7cm) in from the outside edge of the batting and backing, and stitch with a ¼" (7mm) seam. Cut the binding strips 2½" (6.5cm) wide. Place the folded binding strips ⅝" (1.7cm) in from the outside edges, and stitch the binding ⅛" (3mm) out from the previous stitching line, using the inside edge of the ¼" (7mm) foot for accuracy. Trim the quilt sandwich to ½" (1.3cm) from the binding stitching line. Turn the binding to the back of the quilt. Stitch in place.

COLOR PLAY by Gloria Loughman

Finished size: 16¼″ × 20¾″ (41.3cm × 52.7cm)

This is another project that's perfect for practicing more embellishing appliqué and stitching techniques.

Fabric Requirements

Refer to the codes printed on the pattern for fabric placement.

Fabric 1 (*F1, multicolored fabric*): ½ yard (50cm)

Fabric 2 (*F2, orange marbled fabric*): ⅔ yard (60cm)

Fabric 3 (*F3, navy fabric*): ¼ yard (25cm)

Fabric 4 (*F4, orange and turquoise hand-dyed fabric*): ½ yard (50cm)

Fabric 5 (*F5, dark turquoise marbled fabric*): ⅔ yard (60cm)

Fabric 6 (*F6, navy and yellow fabric*): ⅓ yard (30cm)

Fabric 7 (*F7, bright yellow fabric*): ⅛ yard (12cm)

Backing and facing: 1 yard (1m). Cut backing 22″ × 26″ (56cm × 66cm).

Other Supplies

Freezer paper: 1½ yards (1.5m)

Tear-away stabilizer: 1 yard (1m) of 40″ (100cm) wide tear-away or similar fabric stabilizer

Paper-backed fusible web: 1½ yards (1.5m) Wonder-Under, Steam-A-Seam, Vliesofix, or similar product

Batting: 22″ × 26″ (56cm × 66cm)

Invisible thread: nylon or polyester

Thread to match fabrics

Construction

PREPARATION

Use the project pattern from the pullout at the back of the book, and refer to pages 36–37 to create the tear-away stabilizer base, the freezer paper patterns, and the fabric backgrounds for all the segments. Include the extra tear-away stabilizer layer for segments that will be embellished. The sample project shown has all the segments embellished. Staystitch each segment, and remove the freezer paper.

CIRCLES APPLIQUÉ: SEGMENT 1

To make the stitching process for the circle motifs more manageable, create and stitch the circles separately before fusing them in place on the background fabric of Segment 1.

1. Trace the circles and the inner circle motifs onto paper-backed fusible web. Cut them out with a ¼″ (7mm) margin, and then press them to the back of the selected fabric. Cut out following the design drawn on the paper-backed fusible web. Remove the backing paper on the inner circle motifs only, and fuse in place on the circles.

2. Remove the fusible web backing paper from the circles, and place the circles on a piece of tear-away stabilizer that is slightly larger than the circle. Stitch around the inner circle motif, close to the edge.

3. Remove the tear-away stabilizer from the circles, and place them in position on the background fabric of Segment 1. Fuse them in place, then satin stitch. For information on satin stitch and other alternatives, see pages 67–72.

 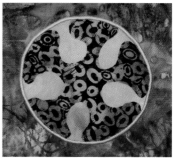

EDGE TREATMENTS: SEGMENTS 2 AND 8

Use the techniques outlined on pages 46–47 to complete these segments. When stitching in place, use free-motion stitching to add a line of straight stitches close to the jigsaw edge. When cutting out the edge treatment shapes, remember to add the seam allowance along the edges where the appliquéd shape meets the segment edge and to turn the segment over and restitch the line of stay stitching through to the front after completion.

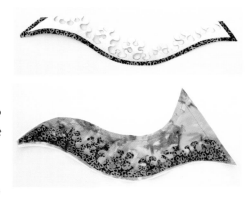

SMALL TRIANGLES: SEGMENTS 3 AND 6

Use the techniques outlined on page 45 to complete these segments. Stitch around each triangle using a triple or straight stitch.

EDGE TREATMENTS PLUS APPLIQUÉ MOTIFS: SEGMENTS 4 AND 9

Use the techniques outlined on pages 46–48 to create the appliqué motifs located on the segment edges. Remember to add a seam allowance along these edges. Fuse circle appliqués in place to complete these segments. Satin stitch around the outsides of the circles. Straight stitch the other parts of the motif.

APPLIQUÉ MOTIFS: SEGMENT 7

For the Segment 7 motifs, use the techniques described for Segment 1.

STRAIGHT STRIPS: SEGMENT 5

Iron fusible web to the back of the strip fabric. Rotary cut strips ¼" (7mm) wide, and place them across the segment as shown on the pattern. Overlap the stay stitching and trim. Stitch along each side of the strips using a triple stitch or straight stitch.

Putting the Segments Together

Remove the tear-away stabilizer from the back of each segment. Refer to pages 37–41 to put all the segments together, stitching them sequentially. Remember to clip the curves as needed.

Finishing

Refer to Borders, Quilting, and Bindings (pages 76–83). This project has a faced edge made from strips cut 3" wide.

Project 3:
Mosaic Appliqué

DAPPLED FOREST by Gloria Loughman

Finished size: 22¾" × 28½" (57.8cm × 72.4cm)

Try your hand at mosaic and other appliqué techniques in this small wallhanging.

Fabric Requirements

8 fabrics that vary in color, pattern, and value: ¼ yard (25cm), ⅛ yard (13cm), or a fat quarter of each

Narrow inner border: ¼ yard (25cm)

Wide outer border: ½ yard (50cm)

Backing: 27″ × 33″ (68.6cm × 83.8cm)

Binding: 12″ × 40″ (30.5cm × 101.6cm)

Other Supplies

Freezer paper: 1 yard (1m)

Tear-away stabilizer: 1 yard (1m) of 40″ (100cm) wide tear-away or similar fabric stabilizer

Paper-backed fusible web: 1 yard (1m) Wonder-Under, Steam-A-Seam, Vliesofix, or similar product

Batting: 27″ × 33″ (68.6cm × 83.8cm)

Invisible thread: nylon or polyester

Thread to match fabrics

Construction

PREPARATION

Use the project pattern from the pullout at the back of the book, and refer to pages 36–37 to create the tear-away stabilizer base, the freezer paper patterns, and the fabric backgrounds for all the segments. For Segments 3, 4, 7, 15, and 19, include the extra tear-away stabilizer layer, as these segments will be embellished. Staystitch these segments, and remove the freezer paper.

The remaining segments are not embellished in the sample. If you decide to add appliqué or extra stitching, place these segments on a layer of tear-away stabilizer before stitching.

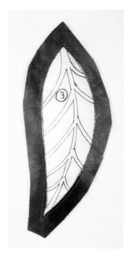 

APPLIQUÉ: SEGMENTS 3, 7, 15, AND 19

Use the techniques outlined on pages 43–47 to complete these segments. Remember to add a seam allowance where the shapes overlap the segment edges.

Segment 3   Segment 15

MOSAIC APPLIQUÉ: SEGMENT 4

Use the techniques outlined on pages 53–55 to complete this segment.

Remember to number each tile so you can reposition the tiles in order, and to stay inside the stay-stitched line. Stitch around each tile in a matching thread using a straight or triple stitch.

Putting the Segments Together

Remove any tear-away stabilizer from the back of segments. Refer to pages 37–41 to put all the segments together. For this project, roughly position all the segments on the tear-away stabilizer base, checking that you are happy with your fabric choices and design.

Finishing

Refer to Borders, Quilting, and Bindings (pages 76–83). This project has a narrow inner border that finishes to ¼" (7mm) wide, using strips that are cut 1¼" (2.2cm) wide, and a wide outer border using strips that are cut 4" (10cm) wide. The binding strips are cut 3½" (9cm) wide.

Project 4:
Abstract Landscape

VILLAGE STRATA by Gloria Loughman

Finished size: approximately 16½″ × 24¼″ (42cm × 61cm)

This abstract landscape features appliqué, curved piecing, and foundation techniques.

Fabric Requirements

SEGMENT 1

Sky (*pale blue-green fabric*): ¼ yard (25cm)

Buildings (*dark violet fabric*): ¼ yard (25cm)

SEGMENT 2

Background (*green fabric*): ¼ yard (25cm)

Jigsaw shape (*yellow-green fabric*): ¼ yard (25cm)

SEGMENT 3

Background (*dark multicolored fabric*): ¼ yard (25cm)

Circles (*green and violet fabric*): ⅛ yard (10cm)

SEGMENT 4

4–7 different fabrics that blend from green to violet: ⅛ yard (10cm) of each

SEGMENT 5

5 different green and violet fabrics: ⅛ yard (10cm) of each (most of the fabrics used in Segment 4 can be repeated in this segment)

Narrow border: ¼ yard (25cm) pale green fabric

Backing: ½ yard (50cm)

Binding: ½ yard (50cm) mottled purple fabric

Other Supplies

Freezer paper: 1 yard (1m)

Tear-away stabilizer: 1 yard (1m) of 40" (100cm) wide tear-away or similar fabric stabilizer

Paper-backed fusible web: ½ yard (50cm) Wonder-Under, Steam-A-Seam, Vliesofix, or similar product

Batting: 18" × 26" (46cm × 66cm)

Invisible thread: nylon or polyester

Thread to match fabrics

Construction

PREPARATION

Use the project pattern from the pullout at the back of the book, and refer to pages 36–37 to create the tear-away stabilizer base, the freezer paper patterns, and the fabric backgrounds for Segments 1, 2, 3, and 4. Include the extra tear-away stabilizer layer, as these segments will be embellished. Staystitch each segment, and remove the freezer paper.

EDGE TREATMENTS: SEGMENTS 1 AND 2

Use the techniques outlined on pages 46–48 to complete these segments. Remember to add a seam allowance where the appliquéd shape meets the edge of the segment. When stitching the edge treatments in place, use a straight or triple stitch, or free-motion stitch to the curves. When complete, turn the segment to the back, and re-stitch the guideline of stay stitching through to the front.

Outline the buildings in a contrasting thread, and, if needed, draw guidelines on the buildings for the stitching lines.

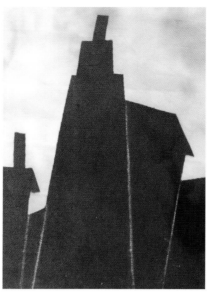

APPLIQUÉ: SEGMENT 3

Use the techniques outlined on pages 44 and 72 to complete this segment. Use a double blanket stitch around the edges of the circles.

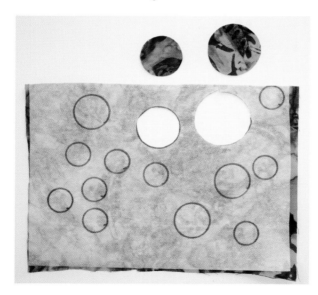

CURVED PIECING: SEGMENT 4

1. Trace the pattern onto tear-away stabilizer.

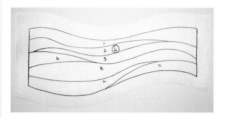

2. Cut out the 7 freezer paper shapes for this segment. With the shiny side down, iron the freezer paper shapes to the right sides of the corresponding fabrics. Cut out Shape 1 with a ½″ (1.3cm) seam allowance around each edge. Cut out Shapes 2 through 7 with a ¼″ (7mm) seam allowance on the top edge and a ½″ (1.3cm) allowance on the side and bottom edges.

3. Place Shape 1 in position using the drawn lines on the tear-away base as a guide. Pin.

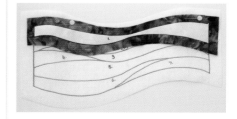

4. Press under the top edge of Shape 2, clipping curved edge where necessary (see page 38). Pin in position on the tear-away base, overlapping Shape 1. Remove the freezer paper. Pin, and stitch with an invisible blind hem stitch (pages 39–41).

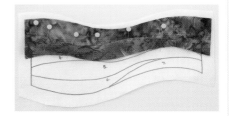

5. Continue to add subsequent shapes, stitching each one down with an invisible blind hem stitch.

6. Turn the segment over, and stitch ⅛″ (3mm) outside the drawn outline for this segment.

FOUNDATION PIECING: SEGMENT 5

Trace Segment 5 onto a piece of tear-away stabilizer following the directions in Foundation Piecing (pages 58–59). Cut out the 12 freezer paper shapes and iron the shiny side to the right side of the selected fabrics, leaving a ½″ (1.5cm) seam allowance around all the edges. Sequentially position and stitch the shapes on the tear-away stabilizer, then stitch ⅛″ (3mm) outside the drawn line of the segment.

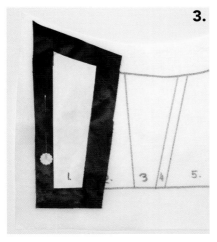

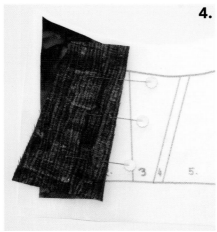

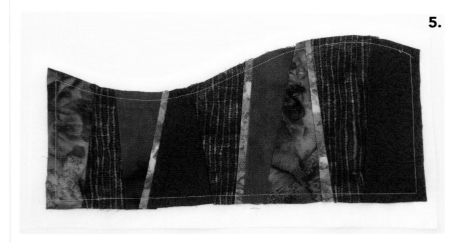

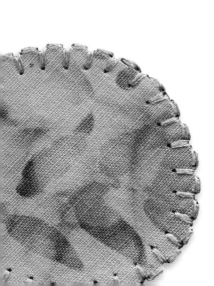

Putting the Segments Together

Remove any tear-away stabilizer from the back of segments. Refer to pages 37–41 to put all the segments together. Remember to clip the curves as needed. Square up the completed quilt top.

Finishing

Refer to Borders, Quilting, and Bindings (pages 76–83). Cut the backing and batting 3½" (8.9cm) wider and longer than the quilt top. Sandwich the quilt, leaving a 1¾" (4.4cm) margin of backing and batting around the edges of the quilt top. Quilt as desired. This project has a narrow inner border ⅛" (3mm) wide, using strips that are cut 1¼" (3.1cm) wide, placed 2" (5cm) in from the outside edges of the sandwich, and stitched with a ¼" (7mm) seam allowance. Trim the batting and backing so the outside edge is 2" (5cm) from the stitched seam for the narrow border. Cut binding strips 8½" (22cm) wide. Fold and press the strips, and place the raw edges of the binding 1¾" (4.4cm) in from the edge. Turn the quilt over, and, using the narrow border stitching line as a guide, sew the bindings on ⅛" (3mm) from this line. Turn and stitch the binding to the quilt back.

Resources

FABRIC PAINT

Hi Strike fabric paint:

Batik Oetoro
www.dyeman.com

Setacolor fabric paint:

Pro Chemical and Dye
www.prochemical.com

Dharma Trading Co.
www.dharmatrading.com

HAND-PAINTED FABRIC

Skydyes, Mickey Lawler
www.skydyes.com

THREAD

The Thread Studio, Perth, Australia
www.thethreadstudio.com

Superior Threads
www.superiorthreads.com

EXTRA-WIDE FREEZER PAPER AND 3-IN-1 COLOR TOOL

C&T Publishing, Inc.
www.ctpub.com

TIPS AND TECHNIQUES

Go to www.ctpub.com >
Consumer Resources >
Tips & Techniques for Quiltmaking
& More >
"Completing a binding with an
invisible seam" (CTPubBlog; March
23, 2009. C&T Publishing, Inc.)

About the Author

Gloria Loughman lives by the sea on the beautiful Bellarine Peninsula in Victoria, Australia. Married with three daughters, she is a trained secondary teacher having worked mainly in the literacy and special education faculties. Her initiation into the world of patchwork occurred approximately twenty years ago, when she was recovering from surgery and chemotherapy for breast cancer.

Over the years she has dabbled in many areas, including strip piecing, bargello, colorwash, fabric dyeing and painting, machine embroidery, and landscape. After completing some studies in design and color as part of a diploma of art in 1996, she began to make large vivid landscape quilts depicting the Australian bush. These quilts have won many major awards in Australia, Europe, Japan, and the United States. Her quilt *Kimberley Mystique* was the winner of Australia's most prestigious national quilting award in 2003.

Gloria loves sharing her knowledge and skills with others. Known to take people outside their comfort zone, Gloria is adept at pushing boundaries while still managing to instill confidence. Many students come back for a second or third class. Gloria's commitment to teaching was acknowledged by her receiving the 2009 Rajah Award for her outstanding contribution to quiltmaking in Australia.

As well as being in demand as a teacher, Gloria has curated eight exhibitions of Australian quilts in the United States and has had the privilege of judging at many major shows. Her quilts have been featured in many books and magazines.

What began as a therapy has developed into a passion and has given Gloria the opportunity to travel the world exhibiting her quilts, teaching classes, and meeting many wonderful people.

Gloria's website: www.glorialoughman.com

Also by Gloria Loughman

Great Titles *from* C&T PUBLISHING

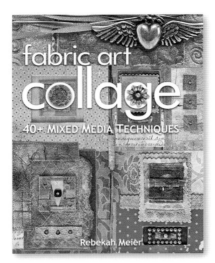

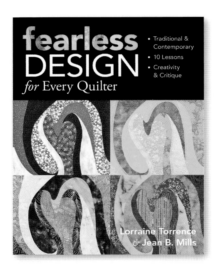

Available at your local retailer or **www.ctpub.com** *or* **800-284-1114**

*For a list of other fine books from C&T Publishing, visit our website to view
our catalog online:*

C&T PUBLISHING, INC.
P.O. Box 1456
Lafayette, CA 94549
800-284-1114

Email: ctinfo@ctpub.com
Website: www.ctpub.com

*C&T Publishing's professional photography services are now available to
the public. Visit us at www.ctmediaservices.com.*

Tips and Techniques *can be found at www.ctpub.com > Consumer
Resources > Quiltmaking Basics: Tips & Techniques for Quiltmaking & More*

For quilting supplies:

COTTON PATCH
1025 Brown Ave.
Lafayette, CA 94549
Store: 925-284-1177
Mail order: 925-283-7883

Email: CottonPa@aol.com
Website: www.quiltusa.com

*Note: Fabrics used in the quilts shown may not be currently
available, as fabric manufacturers keep most fabrics in print for
only a short time.*